Predictive Medicine

Predictive Medicine

Artificial Intelligence and Its Impact on Health Care Business Strategy

Emmanuel Fombu MD, MBA

BEP BUSINESS EXPERT PRESS

Predictive Medicine: Artificial Intelligence and Its Impact on Health Care Business Strategy

First published in 2020 by
Business Expert Press, LLC
222 East 46th Street, New York, NY 10017
www.businessexpertpress.com

ISBN-13: 978-1-63742-367-7
ISBN-13: 978-1-95152-705-1 (e-book)

Business Expert Press Health Care Management Collection

Collection ISSN: 2333-8601 (print)
Collection ISSN: 2333-861X (electronic)

Cover and interior design by Exeter Premedia Services Private Ltd., Chennai, India

First edition: 2020

10 9 8 7 6 5 4 3 2 1

Abstract

Artificial intelligence, machine learning and other new technologies are ready to revolutionize the healthcare industry. But if we want them to achieve their full potential, we'll need leaders who understand these new tools.

Predictive Medicine makes AI more accessible for healthcare practitioners without shying away from complex topics and controversial subject matter. It's a call-to-action for a new generation of health leaders and a roadmap to a brighter future.

Keywords

artificial intelligence; ai; machine learning; ml; technology; technologies; healthcare; health care; health; healthtech; health technology; natural language processing; nlp; robotics; big data; data; personalized healthcare; personalized healthcare; future of healthcare; voice; voice recognition; future; futurism; prediction; medicine; digital; digital health; venture capital; vc; digital therapeutics

Contents

Acknowledgments

First and foremost, thanks are due to my beloved grandmother Jacqueline Nkamanyi (Mami Jaco) for teaching me the importance of education. Thanks are also in order for my family (Martina, Yves, Elise, Irene, Anne Marie, and Mario) for all the support, patience, and guidance while writing this book. Thanks also to my mother (Dr. Regina Nkamanyi) for shaping my medical career and to Anil Moolchandani from Cornell University for first introducing me to the power of big data and artificial intelligence.

I also owe a big debt of thanks to everyone who read my first book, *The Future of Healthcare: Humans and Machines Partnering for Better Outcomes*, and in particular to those who shared feedback or recommended the book to their friends and family. You know who you are.

I would also like to thank everyone who took the time to talk to me throughout the creation of this book. Thanks also to my publishing team, starting with Dane Cobain, my editor, who helped me to shape my manuscript into the book that you are holding in your hands.

Finally, thanks to you, the reader. The future of healthcare is coming—but only if you help to make it happen.

Over to you.

Introduction

Picture the Scene: You just got home from work and your significant other is alone in the kitchen preparing dinner. You hear a command, "Alexa, open all recipes." Your mind starts wandering: mac and cheese… pizza…chicken alfredo…too complicated. But before you're done contemplating, a virtual assistant called Alexa casually spurts out a response: "Welcome back to 'All Recipes.' What do you want to search for?" To which your significant other responds: "Alexa, what can I make with chicken and mushrooms?" This is, of course, what they found in the refrigerator. Alexa then responds, "My recommendation is chicken with mushrooms. It's 4.5 out of 5 stars with thousands of reviews and takes 45 minutes." Forty-five minutes can seem like an eternity when you're hungry. So, your significant other says, "Alexa, I only have 30 minutes." To which Alexa responds, "By setting the time to 30 minutes, I found a Chicken Mushroom Dijon recipe." Your significant other is thrilled and responds, "Alexa, perfect. Start cooking."

If this scenario doesn't sound familiar, then it will before you know it. Alexa is Amazon's artificial intelligence (AI) based virtual personal assistant that interprets natural language and provides answers to questions at lightning speed. Alexa is the chef soulmate you never knew you wanted.

AI is all around us. It's in our phones, cars, watches, banks, hospitals, home security cameras, lightbulbs, computers, shops and dating apps. As a consequence, it's not shocking that investors, corporate executives, managers, CEOs, vice presidents, doctors, lawyers, nurses, policy makers and entrepreneurs are eager to learn about AI: they all recognize that it's going to drastically change the way they've been doing business.

As a business-savvy physician, healthcare futurist, clinical trialist, entrepreneur and staunch advocate for value-based healthcare, I view the advances in AI from a unique perspective. Over the years, I've come to realize that there's a huge knowledge gap in the healthcare industry, particularly when it comes to healthcare leaders and executives and their understanding of AI and machine learning. For AI to achieve its full potential in the field of healthcare, we'll require leaders who understand the technology and have a long-term strategy in place to take advantage of it.

From an economics point of view, for an AI to deliver value in healthcare, it has to drive down costs and improve outcomes. Today, patients wait for symptoms of disease to develop before seeing a healthcare practitioner, at which point it might be too late to treat. AI opens the door to an era of predictive medicine. An era in which disease is prevented, intercepted or cured early.

Throughout my career, I've been working on disruptive new technologies and identifying ways to bring them into the healthcare industry. I've also been fortunate to engage with top AI researchers in the world such as Elon Musk's AI advisor and MIT's Max Tegmark, and I've advised many healthcare start-ups, health systems, and investors, as well as the governments of the United States, the United Arab Emirates, Rwanda, and Austria. Being so close to so many healthcare applications of AI and working for hospitals, start-ups, investment firms, and giants in the pharmaceutical industry such as Bayer, Novartis, and Johnson & Johnson has forced me to think about how this incredible technology affects healthcare business strategy. As I'll explain, AI is a prediction technology. Predictions are inputs to decision making and economics and the practice of medicine provides an excellent framework for understanding the trade-offs that underlie any decision. So, by dint of luck and some design, I find myself at the right place at the right time to form a bridge connecting technologists, hospital systems, payers, patients, pharmaceutical companies, investors, start-ups, and other stakeholders in the business of healthcare.

It's worth understanding that artificial intelligence doesn't actually bring us intelligence but is instead a critical component of intelligence-prediction. In our earlier scenario, what Alexa was doing when your "significant other" posed a question was taking the sounds it heard and then predicting what information the words were looking for. Alexa doesn't know what Chicken Mushroom Dijon tastes like. However, she's able to predict that when someone asks such a question, they're looking for a specific response: a recipe that includes the words "chicken" and "mushrooms." Every decision in healthcare—or in any other business—is based on making the most of a better prediction. Companies such as Brendan Frey's Deep Genomics bring value to medicine by predicting what will happen in a cell when DNA is altered. The Apple Watch improves healthcare by being able to predict the risk of atrial fibrillation or stroke on the wearer, thereby calling for early medical intervention. This adds value to healthcare and all stakeholders stand to benefit. I've also worked on projects in which we were able to successfully predict the risk of suicide and depression based on an individual's voice and to diagnose variations of multiple sclerosis based on changes in MRI imaging over time coupled with changes in activity and sleep.

There's never been a more opportune time for us to tap into the capabilities of artificial intelligence. After all, the healthcare industry is at risk of buckling under its own weight, and patients are expressing their unhappiness with the current system. This is highlighted in *The Employee Experience* by Jacob Morgan, where the author explains, "A survey by PwC of more than 2,300 healthcare patients found that only half were satisfied with their overall experience as healthcare consumers. Ominously (for insurance companies, anyway), many were willing to try nontraditional sources for health insurance, including large retailers (40% of respondents) and digital companies like Amazon (37%)."[1]

For anyone well versed in the world of digital health and innovation, it will come as no surprise that despite the buzz around artificial intelligence in the healthcare industry, business leaders and investors struggle to identify the right business strategy. That's why I decided to write *Predictive Medicine: The Economics of Artificial Intelligence and Its Impact on Healthcare Business Strategy*, which brings together my experience in AI, data science, business, medicine, clinical research, and the healthcare industry. This book is a call-to-action for a new generation of health leaders and a roadmap to help them usher in a brighter future.

When writing this book, my goal was to create a resource to help healthcare industry leaders understand artificial intelligence (AI) and the way it can be used to revolutionize healthcare. As AI technology develops, you can expect to see plenty of new revenue opportunities in the healthcare market, and I like to think of it as a win/win situation. It can make

---

[1] See: http://amzn.to/employeeexperiencebook

money for investors, entrepreneurs, and corporations whilst simultaneously helping patients to live better, healthier lives.

I've tried to make artificial intelligence more accessible for healthcare stakeholders without shying away from complex topics and controversial subject matter. This book doesn't pull any punches. Instead, it aims to be a valuable resource for the years to come.

If you're a business leader, this book aims to provide you with an understanding of the impact of AI on healthcare management and strategy. If you're a student or a recent graduate, this book will give you a framework or roadmap for thinking about the evolution of jobs and future careers in the healthcare industry. If you're an angel investor, analyst, or venture capitalist, this book offers a solid foundation upon which you can build your investment hypothesis. If you're a health policy leader, this book serves as a roadmap for understanding how AI is likely to transform the healthcare environment and how policy could mold those changes for the better.

I hope by the end of this book, you'll be a different person in a number of ways. First, you'll know a lot more about AI in the healthcare industry. You'll be able to describe a number of applications of AI, including machine learning, robotics, and natural language processing. You'll also be able to describe some of the technical, strategic, and other factors to consider when deciding where different kinds of AI applications would be appropriate in the business of healthcare. Moreover, you'll have several ideas and a solid plan for how your own organization or some other entity could leverage AI to gain a strategic advantage.

Secondly, you'll know more about AI generally. I hope that you'll share my view that AI, in the next decade or three or more, won't resemble the scary robots of science fiction. That most kinds of artificial intelligence generated in the near future won't be AI alone, but humans and machines partnering for better outcomes—*augmented intelligence*. I also hope to convince you that AI won't take away your job and if it does, you'll most likely get a more rewarding one. Last but not least, if you're terrified of AI now, my hope is that by the end of this book, you won't be any longer.

To get the most out of this book, I recommend gathering your team together to discuss your AI strategy and ensuring that every team member understands how this exciting new technology will affect their job, the company, and the industry as a whole. But before you get carried away, remember to ask yourself: What problem am I trying to solve and is AI the right tool? AI isn't the solution to every business problem, but it's an incredible tool to have when solving the right business problem. Feel free to share your copy of the book with team members (or better still, buy a copy for each of them) and make sure that it's always available as a reference tool in the workplace.

In the meantime, settle in, get comfortable, and prepare to see the future. It might not be as far away as you think.

Emmanuel Fombu

Emmanuel Fombu, MD, MBA
November 18, 2019

CHAPTER 1

An Introduction to Artificial Intelligence

There is no Reason and no Way that a Human Mind can Keep up With an Artificial Intelligence Machine By 2035.

—*Gray Scott*

Once in a Generation

A breakthrough changes the entire scientific landscape. In the 1940s, it was the Manhattan Project that helped open up the secrets of the atom. In the 1960s, it was the race to the moon that opened up space travel. In the early 2000s, it was the Human Genome Project that determined the sequence of the nucleotide base pairs that make up human DNA as well as identifying and mapping all the genes of the human genome from both a physical and a functional standpoint.

I like to divide the history of medicine intro four eras:

1. *BG: Before the genome*
2. *AG: After the genome*
3. *BA: Before artificial intelligence (AI)*
4. *AA: After AI*

To me, the Human Genome Project marks the transition from the age of discovery to the age of mastery. Having unraveled the fundamental code of our biology, the stage is set for us to manipulate and proactively make sense of it. The biomolecular revolution has begun and is changing everything, including modern medicine. Medicine has gone through at least four basic stages.

The Germ Era (16th Century Onward)

The germ theory was first proposed by Girolamo Francastoro in 1546, although it took some time before it gained widespread acceptance. The germ theory is what led to us improving sanitation and hygiene standards and, ultimately, creating modern sewage systems.

The Antibiotic Era (20th Century)

Most notable for the development and use of penicillin, the antibiotic era allowed us to start vaccinating people against illnesses and to carry out modern surgery.

The Genome Era (Early 21st Century)

The genome era marks the beginning of contemporary medicine, and I like to split it into two eras: BG and AG. For me, the Human Genome Project marks the transition from BG to AG as we went from discovery to mastery. Having unraveled the fundamental code of our biology, the stage is set for us to manipulate and proactively make sense of it. The biomolecular revolution has begun and it is starting to change everything, including modern medicine. As far back as 2000, the then-president Bill Clinton even went on record to say, "Genome science will have a real impact on all of our lives and even more on the lives of our children."

The AI Era (Late 21st Century)

As with the previous era, this can be separated into two subcategories: BA and AA. We are currently in the BA days, at least when it comes to the full potential impact of artificial intelligence in the healthcare industry. When we reach the AA stage, we will see the most profound change of all as the healthcare system embraces the power of genetic medicine beyond the genes. AI technology has been around in the healthcare industry since the 1950s, but it will only be in the coming years that its true impact is felt across the healthcare industry and beyond.

Our modern healthcare is more advanced than it has ever been before, but that does not make it perfect. There are plenty of problems with it, like the fee-for-service system, which has led to a transactional type of healthcare in which people wait to get sick before being treated instead of heading illness off at the pass. At the same time, healthcare costs are going through the roof, and physicians are struggling to spend enough time with their patients.

A classic example of how AI can take an existing problem in the healthcare industry and turn it into advantage is the way we handle electronic health records (EHRs). At the moment, physicians are spending more time filling out patients' health records than they are providing face-to-face care. If AI can take this task on under the oversight of qualified physicians, it would free up that time and allow doctors to spend twice as much time with their patients. To look at it from another perspective, that would have the same impact on face-to-face time as more than doubling our current number of healthcare practitioners.

I like to think that AI is the great predictor, especially because it tends to get better at making its predictions over time. This is good news because the next stage of healthcare, a more personalized stage, requires predictive medicine and value-based healthcare, and AI might be the tool we need to deliver that.

At its most basic level, AI is any form of intelligence that is displayed by machines. The idea is to differentiate between intelligence shown by animals and human beings and intelligence shown by computers. True general AI is almost impossible to achieve, especially with today's technology, which is why AI technologies typically work by mimicking the way that a human mind works. Developers are focusing on creating the infrastructure that will power virtual cognitive functions, such as the ability to perceive, understand, calculate, express, and remember. AI technology differs from regular computer software because of its ability to mimic human reasoning, as well as to create things and to solve problems. A great example of a creative AI is Amper, which powered the first ever music album that was entirely composed and produced by AI software.[1]

---

[1] See: http://bit.ly/firstaialbum

Unlike other forms of computer software, AI is not static and does not just follow pre-set rules that were laid down by a programmer. It is designed to learn and to think, just like a person does, and that is what makes it so powerful. After all, our ability to learn, think, and arrive at conclusions is what makes human beings so versatile and creative. We spend the first years of our life learning in schools and colleges, and we absorb complex ideas and concepts by reading books and watching films. We learn to express ourselves through speech and art forms like writing and making music, and gain the ability to solve problems or draw new conclusions through trial and error.

When we look at other human beings, we are looking at the end result of a long learning process. The intelligence that we display as a species, and which we often cite as the factor that makes us different from machines and other animals, is only possible because of millions of years of evolution.

The process of learning something usually starts with specific examples that we can then generalize and turn into knowledge that can be applied more broadly. This is especially true in today's day and age, when there is no real need for us to memorize lists of presidents by rote when we can just look them up on our smartphones. Instead of just memorizing information, we are focusing more and more on learning theory that can then be applied in practice.

This concept is what makes AI different to traditional computing, because it does not just respond to a pre-defined input with a pre-defined output. Instead, it *learns* like we do, but on top of that, it also has the ability to process information and to come to conclusions much faster than any human being ever could. And, when we combine the promise of AI with Internet connectivity, big data, and the fact that computers do not get tired or forget things, you can start to see why AI has the potential to change the world.

"Your smartphone, house, bank and car already use AI on a daily basis," explain Facebook engineering leads Yann LeCun and Joaquin Quiñonero Candela.

Sometimes it is obvious, like when you ask Siri to get you directions to the nearest gas station, or when Facebook suggests a friend for you to tag in an image you posted online. Sometimes less so, like when you use your Amazon Echo to make an unusual purchase on your credit card and get a fraud alert from your bank. AI is going to bring about major shifts in society through developments in self-driving cars, medical image analysis, better medical diagnosis, and personalized and predictive medicine. It will also be the backbone of many of the most innovative apps and services of tomorrow.[2]

Humans and Machines

Humans and machines both have their advantages, and the best possible approach is to have the two of them working together. Machines tend to be better at jobs that require memorization, data processing, calculation, and mathematical problem-solving. Humans, on the other hand, are better at creative jobs like writing, imagining, reasoning, and solving abstract problems. Getting a human to remember something or getting a machine to create something can be difficult—and it is also often unnecessary.

That is why most AI developers are focusing on systems that enhance what humans are already doing, taking on repetitive tasks and leaving them free to concentrate on what they are good at—a concept known as *augmented intelligence*. Humans and machines are better together than they can ever be apart. In my last book, *The Future of Healthcare: Humans and Machines Partnering for Better Outcomes,* I explained,

> Chess-playing computers can beat a human player, but computers prefer to retreat, while humans are more stubborn and are better at reading their opponent's weaknesses and evaluating complex patterns. Most people now accept that the best chess player is actually a team of both humans and machines. The same will soon be said about the best clinicians and researchers.

Most AI technology focuses on amplifying our existing cognitive abilities with the unique benefits of digital technology. After all, thanks to

---

[2] See: http://bit.ly/facebookmachinelearningquote

new technologies like cloud storage and the Internet-of-Things, AI has more opportunities than ever before to change the way that we interact with the world around us. And it does not get tired or take lunch breaks, either.

Of course, that does not mean that there are no naysayers out there who see AI as a threat. Elon Musk is one of many thought leaders who are concerned about the growth of AI and its effect on our society. He claims that our attempts to make AI safe have only a 5–10 percent chance of success, and he has also gone on record to say, "The risk of something seriously dangerous happening is in the five year timeframe. 10 years at most."[3] He said that five years ago and so far, nothing serious has happened. But it is not too late.

Not everyone agrees with Musk. Facebook's Mark Zuckerberg famously said that Musk's warnings are *pretty irresponsible*, to which Musk replied that Zuck's understanding is *limited*. What is clear, though, is that as with any form of new technology, we need to be careful with it. The last thing we want to do is to become like Dr. Frankenstein with his uncontrollable monster.

Personally, I am an optimist, and I like to think that AI has the potential to change all of our lives for the better. That said, we also need to be careful with our research and development and to keep a close eye on the rapid pace with which the field is evolving.

Perhaps Musk is right to be afraid, at least to some extent. Historically, humanity has been quick to militarize technology. Dynamite was originally created to blast rock during construction work. Drones could be used in search and rescue operations, but they are all too often used to drop bombs on unsuspecting civilians. And Musk foresees a future in which AI has been militarized, too.

"I keep sounding the alarm bell," he says.

But until people see robots going down the street killing people, they don't know how to react, because it seems so ethereal. Under any rate of advancement in AI, we will be left behind by a lot. The

---

[3]   See: http://bit.ly/elonmusksingularity

benign situation with ultra-intelligent AI is that we would be so far below in intelligence we'd be like a pet or a house cat.[4] [5]

Of course, Musk has also said that he plans to make Mars hospitable by dropping nukes on the surface of the planet, so it remains to be seen whether he is all talk. For my part, I am convinced that the advantages of using AI far outweigh any negatives, and I also know from experience how successful a combination of humans and machines can be.

Part of the reason for that is the ability of AI to free up time by taking on some of the tasks that bog people down. This can cut out the dull, repetitive, brainless work and give us more time to focus on the creative tasks that require a human mind, and this is true at every level of every business in every industry. This could be bad news for people who are just coasting and who do not add any value to the company that they work for, but it is good news for the human race as a whole because it will help ensure that every single one of us is working to our full potential.

AI has many benefits, and I have covered some of them already, most notably its ability to automate tasks and save time and resources. One of the most obvious ways in which it can help us is by reducing the amount of time and effort that is needed to make decisions. In healthcare, this means disease prevention, earlier diagnoses, and faster treatment, making the adoption of AI services a matter of life and death in many cases.

And of course, by making companies more efficient, it can also enable them to invest more of their budget in other areas. This could lead to job creation and enable companies to spend more time on research and development, further helping to drive the healthcare industry into the future.

AI, Machine Learning, and Deep Learning

AI has become something of a buzzword, which is why it is so frequently misunderstood. In particular, I tend to find that people confuse AI with machine learning and deep learning, probably because the three technologies are so similar. Machine learning and deep learning are two

---

[4] See: http://bit.ly/muskhousecat
[5] See: http://bit.ly/dangersofai

different techniques that can be applied to an AI algorithm, and it is not too unusual to see multiple machine learning programs being used in the construction of a single AI solution.

As a general rule, AI is a broad term that encompasses both machine learning and deep learning and refers to any use of computers to mimic the cognitive functions of humans. Machine learning is a subset of AI, in the same way that the World Wide Web is a subset of the Internet. The goal for machine learning is to give machines the ability to process data and to arrive at their own conclusions, tweaking their own algorithms as they *learn* more about the information they are working with.

As for deep learning, Data Science Central explains, "[It] goes yet another level deeper and can be considered a subset of machine learning. The concept of deep learning is sometimes just referred to as 'deep neural networks,' referring to the many lawyers involved. A neural network may only have a single layer of data, while a deep neural network has two or more. The layers can be seen as a nested hierarchy of related concepts or decision trees. The answer to one question leads to a set of deeper, related questions. Deep learning networks need to see large quantities of times in order to be trained. An early example of this is the Google Brain learning to recognize cats after being shown over 10 million images. Deep learning networks don't need to be programmed with the criteria that define items; they're able to identify edges through being exposed to large amounts of data."[6]

One example that I like to use is that machine learning and deep learning could both figure out clinical inefficiencies, but AI could take it to the next level by providing suggestions on how to patch them up. It could even automatically send alerts to relevant staff members or cancel orders when you are overstocking certain supplies. I will talk some more about the differences between AI and machine learning in the next chapter.

We live in an exciting age that is full of opportunities. At the moment, today's hospitals and medical facilities can take advantage of AI technology to become outliers in the industry and to gain an edge on the competition.

---

[6] See: http://bit.ly/datasciencecentraldefinition

But it will not be long until AI is so widespread in the healthcare industry that simply using it will be nothing new. It will become a minimum requirement, and you will be at an insurmountable disadvantage if you do not build it into your healthcare company from the start.

Remember, AI offers a way to re-engage with people through an end-to-end solution. This can be useful for retailers and marketers, but it can also be useful for healthcare providers who want to track people's progress through their facility. One report from the McKinsey Global Institute found that 70 percent of companies will adopt at least one form of AI by 2030.[7] That is seven of every 10 companies in every industry across the globe. Healthcare is just the tip of the iceberg.

On top of that, AI is getting stronger and stronger every day, thanks to the enormous amounts of storage and processing power that the cloud has to offer. The combination of these factors makes it possible to make more and more decisions based on data. This can take the form of autonomous AI systems that interpret data and make decisions in real time, and it can also take the form of human-guided AI that communicates through an interface such as a chat bot.

In the field of healthcare, AI allows physicians to predict the onset of conditions or to use complicated modeling techniques to determine potential treatments. They could even tap into data from personal assistants (i.e., Siri, Alexa) and wearable devices. All of this means better prognoses for patients and more personalized treatments at a lower price.

In the world of healthcare, this could have a profound effect. In fact, we are not far off a future in which AI is so commonplace that people have come to expect it. Like it or not, much of the American healthcare system is based upon the principles of capitalism, and AI gives companies in all industries a competitive advantage. But that advantage only lasts until AI use becomes normal, at which point not using it will make you fall behind.

The Opportunities for AI

Most pieces of AI software fall into one of two categories. They either mimic perception (such as by identifying objects in images, carrying out

---

[7] See: http://bit.ly/aistatsadoption

conversations, or interpreting the world around them) or they mimic analytical thinking (such as by interpreting data, finding patterns, and making predictions). Whatever the case, the aim of the technology is usually to go above and beyond what we are capable of as humans.

The good news is that if AI can take on certain tasks, it frees up human beings to be more strategic and productive. Then the machines can focus on what they are better at, which is typically the process of modeling and understanding data. Machines can carry out predictive analytics and help us look to the future, too.

Another big benefit of using AI is that it can be used to process data from different sources to bring it into a single, cohesive system. In the complex Internet-driven world in which we live, we are all used to using different services (e.g., Gmail, Google, Facebook, and so on) and sharing our data in exchange for access to services. All of this data creates a digital footprint that we can tap into to understand everything from public opinion ahead of elections to latent healthcare data that could change the way that we deliver health services throughout society. I like to think that being able to understand this data will usher in a new era of predictive, preventative, and personalized medicine in which healthcare is individualized and we do not wait for diseases to be a problem before we start to treat them.

In the future, there is no reason why we cannot apply machine learning and predictive analytics to our healthcare system and identify metrics that can be measured over time to determine whether we are progressing in the right direction. Those metrics—and the predictions that machine learning algorithms make based upon the data they have available to them—will help determine which actions we take along the way as we continue to push our society into the future of healthcare.

And remember that AI is able to totally revolutionize the way that we understand and process data, especially at scale. In the healthcare industry, AI-based systems could be used to manage facilities and to allocate resources in real time to make sure that physicians can spend more time doing what they do best: treating their patients. AI is not going to take jobs away from physicians. It is just going to make them better at what they do.

AI relies on data to work, and the two go hand in hand. In fact, AI can make sense of the data in a way that we, as human beings, never could. On top of that, even the most basic AI software is easily capable of automating certain workflows. As long as it is being provided with the information it needs, it should be able to start running analytics and identifying the best actions to take. In a hospital setting, this could include making diagnostic suggestions to save doctors time or finding new efficiencies to reduce wastage and cut down on overheads.

There are alternatives to AI, of course. It is just that quite often, they are not very good. For example, checklists, protocols, and manual processes can all be corrupted by human failures, whereas they are a perfect fit for AI. AI can even bring consistency to your systems and your communications to create a united front for consumers at every touchpoint. And, when it comes to the future of healthcare, the patients are the consumer—and lest we forget, we will all be patients at some point in our lives. It all comes back to the idea of humans and machines partnering for better outcomes. We are better when we work together than we ever are apart. A great example of this from the healthcare industry is the use of AI to power specialist tools for people with disabilities, like a 24/7 companion that never gets tired. It can give them back the power of speech or help them regain their independence. And, when it is coupled with machine learning, it can start to learn more about the specific user and their quirks to improve the results of the software over time.

Precision Medicine

The Precision Medicine Initiative defines precision medicine as "an emerging approach for disease treatment and prevention that takes into account individual variability in genes, environment and lifestyle for each person."[8]

One of the biggest opportunities for AI is its potential to power precision medicine systems and to pioneer a future in which every patient is treated as a true individual. We are already on our way, thanks to private companies like 23AndMe and huge scientific efforts like the Human Genome Project.

Today, you can go to the doctors' office, get a physical exam, receive a clean bill of health, walk out the door, and then suddenly drop down

---

[8] See: http://bit.ly/precisionmedicinedefinition

dead. That is because we are not born with an owners' manual for our body. That seems ridiculous to me, because I have an owners' manual for my laptop, my car, my iPad, and even for my Ikea furniture. I have an owners' manual for just about everything I own, but I do not have one for me. I do not think that is acceptable. And, in the future, I think we will all have a digital file with all of our genes and medical records on it. A great example of this concept in action is Bitmark Health, which describes itself as "a secure, open-source mobile healthcare app that stores your entire health history as a portable and personal health record."[9]

I recently decided to take my first step toward developing my own personal owner's manual, starting with mapping my genetic profile. A simple blood test will reveal whether I carry a gene for Alzheimer's, heart disease, mental illness, diabetes, and other major diseases. Genetic screening can already map out our entire medical makeup, and in the future, it will be as routine as checking our blood pressure.

Until then, I can make a start on my journey into my own personal future, but that could be a double-edged sword. On the one hand, I am a physician scientist, and so I am all in favor of getting to the truth about what is in my genome. At the same time, it could be like lifting the lid on Pandora's Box because all humans have a half dozen or so genes that are screwed up, and in some cases they can even be lethal. Sequencing my genome allows me to see a side of me that I have never seen before, and one which is cause for some anxiety. It is a side of me that could potentially have lurking medical problems. It also opens up questions about data privacy. How can I be sure that the gene testing company will not sell or share my data with a third party without my consent? Luckily, the physician scientist in me won out in the end, and I decided to go for it.

Screening my genetic profile would not have been an option at all without one of the greatest scientific accomplishments in human history: The Human Genome Project. This 13-year project brought scientists and funding together from around the world to sequence the full set of around 30,000 genes that make up human DNA, with the ultimate goal of treating, curing, and even preventing many of the different diseases that plague humanity.

---

[9] See: http://bit.ly/bitmarkhealth

A great example of precision medicine in action comes to us via the Clinic for Special Children (CSC) in Strasburg, Pennsylvania. At the CSC, the clinic routinely examines its patients' DNA and uses genetic testing to offer more personalized care with tangible results. According to Delaware Online, this extends "to the point that a child doesn't suffer from a brain injury or have to depend on a wheelchair."[10]

A few decades ago, it would take 10 years to sequence a human genome. Today, it takes 24 hours, and tomorrow, even less time as the technology improves. The difference in treatment and outcome can be startling. Instead of picking treatments based on the average responses of a large population, doctors can look at one person's genes and decide whether a specific medicine or treatment will be best.

According to Dr. Kevin Strauss, medical director at the CSC, in the not so distant future, clinicians will be able to look at the genetic code of any individual as a vital tool or beacon that allows them to more intelligently, more rationally, and more safely guide every aspect of their care throughout the arc of their lifetime.

Prediction and precision medicine has been especially useful when treating the local Amish population, as they typically intermarry and have genetic differences to the rest of the population that make them more susceptible to certain diseases. Another example is a disorder called *ornithine transcarbamylase deficiency*, an inherited disorder that causes ammonia to accumulate in the blood, leading to severe brain damage if left unchecked. Thanks to genetic testing, physicians can tell whether babies are susceptible and then make recommendations for dietary restrictions and medications that could help stop the disease from progressing. Without this testing, physicians would have waited until the child fell into a coma before they would able to provide a diagnosis.

"The clinic has also been able to reduce a condition called Maple Syrup Urine disease (MSUD) in the Lancaster community by 95%," the report concludes. The condition, which is known for making an infant's urine smell like maple syrup, could lead to seizures and even death, if left untreated. A common form of treatment for MSUD is avoiding foods with a high amount of protein. By catching it in newborns before

---

[10] See: http://bit.ly/precisionmedicinecsc

symptoms appear, the Amish Lancaster community saves about eight million U.S. dollars annually in hospital costs in addition to the countless quality of lives that have been improved and saved.

The Data We Need

Of course, we cannot arrive at informed conclusions without having access to data. A recent report from Orion Health made for particularly interesting reading because it went into specifics when highlighting the types of data that could come in useful for precision medicine.[11]

Social Data

Personal circumstances, such as living situation and income.

Exposome

Impact of the external environment, such as pollution and tobacco smoke.

Device Data

Information collected from apps that measure fitness and sleeping, electronic inhalers, and so on.

Microbiome

The collective name for the 100 trillion microscopic bugs living inside of us all.

Metabolome

Chemicals that are created, modified, and broken down by bodily processes such as enzymatic reactions.

---

[11]   See: http://bit.ly/precisionmedicinereport

Proteome

A system of proteins, including enzymes, which are the building blocks of the body.

Transcriptome

Messages created from DNA to form the template (mRNA) of proteins.

Genome

The patient's complete set of genes as *written* in their DNA.

Epigenetic (Methylome)

The set of nucleic and methylation modifications in a human genome.

Clinical Data

The patient's medical record.

Imaging

Medical images, such as X-rays, scans, and ultrasounds.

Getting hold of all of this data, especially in a single, centralized system, could prove to be almost impossible. If we switch to a decentralized system, we might have a little more luck. Either way, it is not an all-or-nothing situation but rather a case of the more data we have, the better. We will take a further look at the importance of data later on in the book.

AI and VR

AI and machine learning are often used to power virtual reality (VR) solutions, and it is likely that we will find AI, VR, augmented reality (AR), and machine learning all coming closer and closer together as time goes on. This is important because VR and AR are increasingly being seen as potential solutions for everything from pain management to the growing opioid crisis.

Take, for example, Akili Interactive, which has developed a video game for children with Attention Deficit Hyperactivity Disorder, demonstrated a statistically significant improvement in a randomized clinical trial and could one day become the world's first prescription video game.[12]

But my favorite use of VR, at least for now, is the way that it is being used as an alternative to opioids for pain management. Forbes has predicted that the market for VR and AR technology in the healthcare industry will increase to 5.1 billion U.S. dollars by 2025, with 3.4 million patients relying upon it. The article goes on to explain that VR has been shown to *provide meaningful improvements* in five key areas.[13]

Prevention

Promoting wellness and stress management and avoiding addictive behavior.

Pain Management

Distraction experiences as alternatives to providing painkillers.

Training

Clinical skills and surgical skill training in a controlled environment with scenarios that can be repeated as needed.

Adherence

The heightened sense of experience and game-like features of VR help to motive patients and to engage them more fully in their own treatment process.

Telemedicine

Cellphone-based or standalone VR systems could allow physicians to interact with patients virtually, providing healthcare access to underserved

---

[12]   See: http://bit.ly/akiliinteractive
[13]   See: http://bit.ly/forbesvrhealthcare

populations, supporting home recovery, enhancing chronic disease management, and helping the aged.

What I find particularly interesting is their nod to VR's potential to bring people closure. For example, while it might not be possible to take a terminally ill patient on a hot-air balloon ride or to the Niagara Falls, it will be possible for us to simulate it through VR. Sometimes, we as physicians forget that caring for someone requires more than just writing out prescriptions. It is our duty to give people the best quality of life that we can—and then to provide the best quality of death when it comes to it.

High-Performance AI

"Medicine is at the crossroad of two major trends," explains healthcare thought leader Eric J. Topol in an article for *Nature Medicine*.[14]

> The first is a failed business model, with increasing expenditures and jobs allocated to healthcare, but with deteriorating key outcomes, including reduced life expectancy and high infant, childhood and maternal mortality in the United States. The second is the generation of data in massive quantities, from sources such as high-resolution medical imaging, biosensors with continuous output of physiologic metrics, genome sequencing, and electronic medical records.

Topol is a fellow proponent of AI in the healthcare industry, and it is easy to see why. It is the perfect tool to help the healthcare industry to navigate both of the key trends that he highlighted and to drive the industry into the future. Topol says that we are only at the beginning of the AI revolution, and I agree. Still, he highlighted some fascinating uses of AI that I would like to reproduce here.

---

[14] See: http://go.nature.com/highperformancetopol

Radiology

Chest X-rays are by far the most common type of medical scan, with over two billion of them carried out every year across the globe. "In one study," Topol explains, "the accuracy of one algorithm, based on a 121-layer convolutional neural network, in detecting pneumonia in over 112,000 labeled frontal chest X-ray images, was compared with that of four radiologists. The conclusion was that the algorithm outperformed the radiologists."

Pathology

Topol points to a study of breast cancer that compared the performance of 11 pathologists with that of several different algorithms. The results here were less clear cut, providing a timely reminder that we still have a long way to go. "Some of the five algorithms performed better than the group of pathologists, who had varying expertise," Topol explains.

> The pathologists were given 129 test slides and had less than 1 minute for review per slide, which likely does not reflect normal workflow. On the other hand, when one expert pathologist had no time limits and took 30 hours to review the same slide set, the results were comparable with the algorithm for detecting noninvasive ductal carcinoma.

Dermatology

Topol points to a study that used a dataset of nearly 130,000 photographic and dermascopic digitized images. "21 US board-certified dermatologists were at least matched in performance by an algorithm," Topol says,

> which had an [approximate accuracy rate] of 0.96 for carcinoma and 0.94 for melanoma. Subsequently, the accuracy of melanoma skin cancer diagnosis by a group of 58 international dermatologists was compared with a convolutional neural network. The mean [accuracy rates] were 0.79 versus 0.86, respectively, reflect-

ing an improved performance of the algorithm compared with most of the physicians.

Ophthalmology

Topol points to a study of 997 patients with a range of 50 different retinal pathologies, where they were assessed for urgent referral by an algorithm. "The results were compared with those from experts," Topol says.

> Four retinal specialists and four optometrists, with an AUC for accuracy of urgent referral triage to replace false alarm of 0.992. The algorithm did not miss a single urgent referral case. Notably, the eight clinicians agreed on only 65% of the referral decisions.

Cardiology

Topol highlights the case of 267 patient studies (consisting of over 830,000 still images), which were classified into 15 standard views. "The overall accuracy for single still images was 92% for the algorithm and 79% for four board-certified echocardiographers," Topol says. "But this does not reflect the real-world reading of studies, which are in-motion video loops."

Gastroenterology

In the field of gastroenterology, AI was used to find diminutive (i.e., less than 5mm) adenomatous or sessile polyps from colonoscopies. "The first prospective clinical validation of AI was performed in 325 patients who collectively had 466 tiny polyps," Topol explains,

> with an accuracy of 94% and negative predictive value of 96% during real-time, routine colonoscopy. The speed of AI optical diagnosis was 35 seconds, and the algorithm worked equally well for both novice and expert gastroenterologists, without the need for injecting dyes. The findings of enhanced speed and accuracy were replicated in another independent study.

Mental Health

This is an area that I am particularly interested in because at my new role at Johnson and Johnson, I will be working with AI and other emerging technologies to provide new ways of treating patients with mental health disorders. Topol says,

> Various tools that are in development include digital tracking of depression and mood via keyboard interaction, speech, voice, facial recognition, sensors, and use of interactive chat bots. Facebook posts have been shown to predict the diagnosis of depression later documented in electronic medical records. Machine learning has been explored for predicting successful antidepressant medication, characterizing depression, predicting suicide, and predicting bouts of psychosis in schizophrenics.

Inquiries and Initiatives

The good news for healthcare organizations is that there is no shortage of inquiries and initiatives from governments and non-profit organizations that aim to stimulate further thinking about AI across the healthcare industry. Just a few of the most notable include the following.

The Center for Data Ethics and Innovation

This U.K. government initiative was announced in January 2018 and aims to provide advice and guidelines on safe, ethical, and innovative uses of data-driven AI technologies.[15]

Ada Lovelace Institute

Created by the Nuffield Foundation, the Ada Lovelace Institute was set up in 2018 to examine the ethical and social issues that are inherent to the use of data, algorithms, and AI.[16]

---

[15] See: http://bit.ly/dataethicscentre
[16] See: http://bit.ly/adalovelaceinstitute

Partnership on AI

This has been described as "a platform for discussion and engagement around AI founded by Amazon, Apple, DeepMind, Facebook, Google, IBM and Microsoft."[17]

IEEE

The IEEE is the Institute of Electrical and Electronics Engineers, and back in 2016, they launched their Global Initiative on Ethics of Autonomous and Intelligent Systems.[18]

U.S. Government

The U.S. Government has proposed a 215 million U.S. dollar investment in All of Us[19] (formerly known as the Precision Medicine Initiative) and a one billion U.S. dollar investment in Cancer Breakthroughs 2020,[20] which aims to find vaccine-based immunotherapies against cancer.

United Nations: The United Nations Interregional Crime and Justice Research Institute launched a program dedicated to AI and robotics back in 2015.[21]

Asilomar AI Principles: This initiative was created in 2017 by America's Future of Life Institute and was signed by over 3,800 researchers and AI and robotics professionals from around the world. It aims to guide AI research and application in a single, cohesive direction.[22]

---

[17] See: http://bit.ly/partnershiponai
[18] See: http://bit.ly/ieeeinitiative
[19] See: http://bit.ly/allofusinvestment.
[20] See: http://bit.ly/cancerbreakthroughs2020
[21] See: http://bit.ly/unicjriprogram
[22] See: http://bit.ly/asilomaraiprinciples

Other Reports: The Nuffield Council on Bioethics explains,

> Reports on AI have been published by the House of Lords Select
> Committee on Artificial Intelligence, the Royal Society, Reform,
> Future Advocacy and Wellcome, Nesta, and the European Group
> on Ethics in Science and New Technologies. A further report is
> expected from the House of Commons Science and Technology
> Select Committee.[23]

The hope is that by providing this kind of support at a governmental
level, it will be possible to improve overall population health and even to
stimulate the economy. It will also help governments to better understand
these rapidly developing new technologies, which is particularly important because there is currently a lack of legislative oversight.

If legislation is too loose, we risk putting patients and their data in
danger by failing to put adequate safeguards in place. If it is too tight, it
could scupper future development and slow the progress that can already
feel like it is moving at a snail's pace. I do not have all of the answers, but
I think that any inquiries and initiatives that aim to find them are a good
start.

The Bad News

I have been accused of being too optimistic about what the future will
bring, and perhaps with good reason. Personally, I prefer to think of
myself as a realist, and it is certainly true that there are plenty of challenges along the way that could stop us from making the future that we
deserve a reality. The rest of this chapter will be dedicated to addressing a
few of those areas where new technologies have caused unexpected challenges, failed to add value, or even turned out to be outright failures.

One example in the field of machine learning comes to us via a recent
study by Reaction Data, which looked specifically at the fields of radiology and imaging and which aimed to find out where AI could be more
useful to medical professionals. As Healthcare Informatics explained,

---

[23]   See: http://bit.ly/nuffieldbioethics

[The company] got feedback from imaging professionals, including directors of radiology, radiologists, chiefs of radiology, imaging techs, PACS administrators and managers of radiology, from 152 healthcare organizations. About 60% of respondents were from academic medical centers or community hospitals, while 15% were from integrated delivery networks and 12% were from imaging centers. The remaining respondents worked at critical access hospitals, specialty clinics, cancer hospitals or children's hospitals.[24]

The results are illuminating, predictable, and pessimistic in equal measures. The key findings included:

In total, 77% of imaging and radiology leaders view machine learning as being important in medical imaging, up from 65% in 2017. Only 11% view it as unimportant. And, 59% say they understand machine learning, 20% say they do not, and 20% say they have a partial understanding.

In addition, 22% of the respondents are currently using machine learning, while 11% plan to adopt it within the next year. 51% of the respondents say their organizations are 1–2 years (28%) or more than three years (23%) away from adoption. A further 16 % believe that their organizations will never adopt machine learning technology.

Furthermore, 22% of the respondents are using machine learning for breast imaging or lung imaging, followed by cardiovascular imaging (13%), chest X-rays (11%), bone imaging (7%), liver imaging (7%), neural imaging (5%), and pulmonary imaging (4%).

Of the respondents, 19% are using solutions by GE Healthcare, followed by Hologic (16%), Philips (14%), Arterys (7%), Zebra Medical Vision (5%), iCAD (5%), Google (3%), and Nvidia (3%). 14% report using their own homegrown solutions.

All of this goes to show that while machine learning is a promising technology when it comes to the healthcare industry, we have more work to do before it becomes a mainstream solution that is adopted across the board.

---

[24] See: http://bit.ly/reactiondatasurvey

Like I said, I think of myself as a realist, and it seems to me that while we might not be where I would like us to be as an industry, we are at least taking steps in the right direction. In the meantime, it falls to us as forward-thinking supporters of the future of healthcare to continue to encourage the development and adoption of machine learning technologies until they are as common as X-rays and EHRs.

The AI Uprising

Is AI coming to kill us all? Elon Musk certainly thinks so.

True, the enigmatic billionaire and owner of SpaceX and Tesla is not exactly a stranger to outlandish predictions. You might remember when he started his Boring Company virtually on a whim after talking about it on Twitter. You might also remember him claiming that we are all living in a computer simulation like the Matrix and his claim that we can make Mars inhabitable to humans by dropping nukes on it.

Well, Musk is back again, and this time, he claimed that our efforts to make AI safe have only a 5–10 percent chance of success. This comes off the back of a previous prediction in which he said, "The risk of something seriously dangerous happening is in the five year timeframe. 10 years at most." At the time of writing, he made that prediction four years ago and so far, nothing serious has happened. But it is not too late.

Not everyone agrees with Musk. Facebook's Mark Zuckerberg famously said that Musk's warnings are *pretty irresponsible*, to which Musk replied that Zuck's understanding is *limited*. What is clear, though, is that, as with any form of new technology, we need to be careful with it. The last thing we want to do is to become like Dr. Frankenstein with his uncontrollable monster.

Personally, I am an optimist, and I think AI has the potential to change all of our lives for the better. That said, I also think we need to be careful with our research and development and to keep a close eye on the rapid pace with which it is developing.

Perhaps Musk is right to be afraid, at least to some extent. Historically, humanity has been quick to militarize technology. Dynamite was originally created to blast rock during construction work. Drones should be used in search and rescue operations and photography and videography, but they are all too often used to drop bombs on unsuspecting civilians. And Musk foresees a future in which AI has been militarized, too.

"I keep sounding the alarm bell," he says,

> but until people see robots going down the street killing people, they don't know how to react, because it seems so ethereal. Under any rate of advancement in AI, we will be left behind by a lot. The benign situation with ultra-intelligent AI is that we would be so far below in intelligence we'd be like a pet or a house cat.[25] [26]

---

[25] See: http://bit.ly/muskhousecat

[26] See: http://bit.ly/dangersofai

CHAPTER 2

The Dark Side of AI

The upheavals [of artificial intelligence] can escalate quickly and become scarier and even cataclysmic. Imagine how a medical robot, originally programmed to rid cancer, could conclude that the best way to obliterate cancer is to exterminate humans who are genetically prone to the disease.

—*Nick Bilton*

Throughout the majority of this book, and indeed throughout my career, I have focused predominantly on the benefits of artificial intelligence (AI) and new technologies. That is partly because I am an optimist, and partly because I think that obsessing over the drawbacks of new tech could stop us from making advances. I also think that we are still in the early days of AI's implementation era, though the history of AI stretches back at least to the 1960s. Today's cutting-edge health-tech companies are the early innovators, and a certain amount of failure is to be expected. In many ways, it has to happen for healthcare technology to continue to mature.

With that said, I wanted to take some time here to dwell on the more negative aspects of AI so that we can build on them in later chapters. Ultimately, I intend to show that while there are risks involved with pursuing AI, those risks are more than offset by the advantages that these technologies have to share.

The journey toward true AI integration within the healthcare industry will not be an easy one. At the same time, every journey begins with a single step, and if we are to transition from where we are now to where we could (and *should*) be, we need to put one foot in front of the other until we arrive at our destination. From time to time, we might even find ourselves taking a step backward, and that is okay too. As long as we keep on walking and we keep our eyes on the prize, we will get there.

In the meantime, we should not be surprised if we run into a few more problems on the way. One obvious example is IBM's Watson, which essentially overpromised and under-delivered.[1] Doctors have lost faith in it,[2] and IBM has even been accused of distracting from the Watson failure to sell more AI.[3]

In my view, Watson did have a few successes, but those successes just have not been enough to justify the huge investments that the system required. On top of that, the technology has been hit by scandal after scandal, including one instance in which it gave out advice that could have caused cancer patients with severe bleeding to be given drugs that would have caused the bleeding to worsen.[4] And, while this was apparently a hypothetical scenario and did not occur *out in the wild*, it still sheds some light on some of the ways that Watson was not necessarily ideal.

Perhaps, that is why IBM reportedly halted sales of Watson for drug discovery.[5] Last year, the company laid off employees who were working for Watson Health,[6] and Deborah DiSanzo, the former head, left her post after three years.[7] It certainly looks as though unless the company is able to turn things around—and drastically—Watson will go down in history as a failure, or, as I like to think of it, more optimistically, as an early casualty in the battle for better healthcare.

Back in 2013, IBM partnered with the University of Texas MD Anderson Cancer Center as part of *its mission to eradicate cancer*. The problem is that IBM trained the software on a small number of hypothetical cancer patients, rather than on real data.[8] After being described as *a piece of s**t* by one doctor, the project was shelved in February 2017. Later, a report by auditors from the University of Texas found that the MD Anderson Cancer Center had spent 62 million U.S. dollars without achieving their goals.

---

[1]   See: http://bit.ly/watsonspectrum

[2]   See: http://bit.ly/doctorslosingfaith

[3]   See: http://bit.ly/IBMWatsonFail

[4]   See: http://bit.ly/watsonbadrecommendations

[5]   See: http://bit.ly/ibmhaltssales

[6]   See: http://bit.ly/watsonhealthlayoffs

[7]   See: http://bit.ly/disanzoleaves

[8]   See: http://bit.ly/ibmunsafeincorrect

And, it is not just the healthcare industry that has witnessed its fair share of AI fails. For example, there was a case in Germany of an Amazon Echo activating itself in the middle of the night when its owner was not at home. It started blasting out loud music, the neighbors reported it, and the cops broke down the front door to find out what was happening. To add insult to injury, when the man finally got home, he found that they had replaced the door's lock and his key did not work.

Then, there is the case of the researchers who found that they could fool self-driving cars by adding paint or tape to stop signs. By adding the words *love* and *hate* to a stop sign, they managed to convince a self-driving car that it was a *Speed Limit 45* sign in 100 percent of their tests.

Even in the healthcare industry, Watson is hardly the first example of an AI that did not work out. Take MYCIN, a system developed at Stanford in the early 1970s. The goal of the system was to identify which bacteria were causing infections and to recommend antibiotic treatments with a dosage that was tailored toward the patient's weight.

The ironic thing about MYCIN is that, despite being developed all those years ago, it may well have been a better performer. In the abstract for a 1979 paper on MYCIN, authors Victor L. Yu, MD, Lawrence M. Fagan, Sharon M. Wraith et al. explain,

Eight independent evaluators with special expertise in the management of meningitis compared MYCIN's choice of antimicrobials with the choices of nine human prescribers for 10 cases of meningitis. MYCIN received an acceptability rating of 65% by the evaluators; the corresponding ratings for acceptability of the regimen prescribed by the five faculty specialists ranged from 42.5% to 62.5%. The system never failed to cover a treatable pathogen while demonstrating efficiency in minimizing the number of antimicrobials prescribed. The study design may be useful in assessing the performance of other computer-based clinical decision-making systems.[9]

---

[9]   See: http://bit.ly/MYCINpaper

MYCIN was never rolled out to be used in clinical practice, mostly because of a lack of infrastructure at the time. Remember, this was at a time before personal computers were widespread and way before Tim Berners-Lee invented the World Wide Web in 1989. Still, it is an early example of the promise of AI and a reminder that just because an AI program fails now, it does not mean that the idea is not valid. And so, with that in mind, let us take a closer look at a few of the downsides of AI before we focus once more on the benefits that it can bring to the table.

The Challenges of Adopting AI

One of the biggest challenges of adopting AI within the healthcare industry is the fact that AI itself could be at odds with current safety and data laws. In fact, one recent study by *BJM Quality and Safety* aimed specifically to highlight some of the issues that AI and machine learning will come up against.[10] Separated into short-, medium-, and long term, some of those challenges included the following:

Short Term

One of the biggest challenges is the disparity of data and a phenomenon called *distributional shift*, where training data and real-world data are different and, thus, lead to erroneous conclusions. Machine learning algorithms also cannot *err on the side of caution* as humans can.

Medium Term

The idea here is that machine learning and other technologies could lead to us becoming complacent and blindly trusting computer-generated assessments without challenging them. Machine learning could also lead to biases in medical research by making *self-fulfilling predictions*, which might not be the best course of action, but which will reinforce its decision-making process over time.

---

10   See: http://bit.ly/aichallengeshealth

Long Term

While researchers note that we are a long way away from this point, they raise the question of what to do in a hypothetical future where algorithms are in control of equipment that is vital to human life (such as ventilators and life support systems). Unlike human beings, AI systems can only look at the data and are unable to take into consideration the wider context in which any of their decisions are made.

Context

In today's health-tech landscape, we find ourselves at something of a tipping point. We have much of the data that we need and most of the tools to process it, as well as promising new technologies that are showing some early signs of success in clinical trials. But, we still have a long way to go. It is as though we have all of the different parts of the jigsaw, but we have not been able to put them together.

Brigham Hyde, the CEO and co-founder of Precision Health AI, says that AI in healthcare will fail without the proper context. "The systems of making decisions in our sector today are inefficient, full of human flaws and bias," he explains.

> I've come to realize that the problem isn't technology but context. We need to be sharing a vision. We need to be translating information back and forth seamlessly between physicians, researchers, patients and computers to ask better questions and find better answers. The way to bring healthcare leaders together around AI is to invite them in through the proper contextual setting of findings.[11]

This will not be easy, and it will also take time to become a reality. On top of that, there are a huge number of stakeholders involved, and each group will need to be both educated and involved in the process. Hyde suggests focusing on the following:

---

[11] See: http://bit.ly/hydeprecisionhealth

Physicians

AI needs to work within physicians' existing workflows. It is their role to communicate with patients and to put their medical knowledge into context. As AI and machine learning become more and more important in the context of the healthcare industry, physicians will increasingly need to be able to explain these types of technologies to their patients.

Patients

Patients are essentially consumers, and more informed consumers across every industry are already having an impact on how products and services are purchased. The healthcare industry will be no different, and patients will come to expect to be involved in the decision-making process for their treatment plans. They will have the knowledge they need to do it, too.

Payers

"Did the patient get better?" Hyde asks.

> Was the treatment we approved the most cost-effective? Where can we reduce risk while still innovating? Health plans know today's rising health care costs aren't sustainable. Adding the payer context around reimbursement goals into the science can help reduce costs and improve outcomes.

Life Sciences

This mostly comes down to the wider discussion about how AI will affect drug discovery and the process of clinical trials. For example, AI could be used to identify the most viable patients for any given clinical trial with the goal of reducing the chances of adverse effects.

Policymakers

Hyde says,

Regulators play a crucial role in fitting AI into the healthcare ecosystem responsibly. They translate when AI models constitute medical devices and when they should be reimbursable. They will monitor issues around safety, liability and even unintentional bias if models are built on biased data.

Technology

Predictive Medicine Technology leaders will be responsible for their fair share of communication here, too. Hyde says, AI needs to be carefully trained to contextualize results into more practical *so-what* type of actions, and indeed that has been an area that is been lacking in recent years. Let us hope that changes in the near future.

CHAPTER 3

Machine Learning in Healthcare

People worry that computers will get too smart and take over the world, but the real problem is that they're too stupid and they've already taken over the world.

—*Pedro Domingos, Author of The Master Algorithm*

Machine learning and artificial intelligence (AI) are not identical, but they are close relatives. Let us take a look at how the two of them relate before we investigate how machine learning technology can help us to improve our healthcare system.

The big difference between machine learning and AI is that AI systems are designed to mimic intelligent behavior, while machine learning specifically relates to the art and science of getting computers to *learn* and to make deductions without specifically being programmed. An AI-powered chat bot might be able to carry out a conversation, but machine learning would enable it to learn new words and phrases based on the inputs that it receives. It does not always work out for the best, though. Back in 2016, Microsoft released a chat bot called Tay that quickly started spouting racism after picking up a few bad habits from other Twitter users.[1]

Most machine learning software are run via the medium of AI, but the two are not identical. Rather, they are sister technologies that each require a specific set of skills. That is why, major companies like Microsoft, Google, and Apple are hiring both AI specialists and machine learning researchers at an unprecedented rate, with many of them dipping their toes into healthcare as a result of it.

---

[1] See: http://bit.ly/tayrants

And, while all of this is happening, industry pundits are increasingly turning their attention to machine learning as a potential solution to many of the healthcare industry's issues. Nature, the *International Journal of Science*, even has a page on its website, which publishes a continually updated list of research, news, and commentary on the subject of machine learning in healthcare.[2] Recent article titles include *Development and validation of a deep-learning algorithm for the detection of polyps during colonoscopy* and *Explainable machine-learning predictions for the prevention of hypoxaemia during surgery.*

When I talk about AI and machine learning, a lot of people get confused. There still seems to be some uncertainty around the similarities and differences between the two technologies. Fortunately, I recently came across a great article by author Bernard Marr for Forbes in which he explained:

> Artificial intelligence is the broader concept of machines being able to carry out tasks in a way that we would consider "smart." Machine learning is a current application of AI based around the idea that we should really just be able to give machines access to data and let them learn for themselves.

The modern field of machine learning is largely a direct descendent of Arthur Samuel's 1959 realization that, instead of teaching computers everything they need to know about the world and how to interpret it, it might be possible to teach them to learn for themselves. The trial-and-error approach to data processing, made possible by the big data that we store and create, allows computers to *learn* in much the same way that we learn as human beings. And, in the same way that babies learn to listen and speak, Marr explains that "machine learning is [also used] to help machines understand the vast nuances in human language, and to learn to respond in a way that a particular audience is likely to comprehend."

AI, machine learning, and natural language processing used to be the exclusive domain of science fiction writers and technology geeks, but no

---

[2]   See: http://bit.ly/naturemachinelearning

longer. The concepts are starting to play a huge part in our daily life, with entrepreneurs such as Elon Musk and Bill Gates even cautioning that AI could spell the end of the world if we are not careful about its development. Meanwhile, Felix Kjellberg—also known as PewDiePie, the world's most subscribed to YouTuber—recently released a video about AI and machine learning, which picked up over two million views in its first two days. That is one in the eye for those who think AI is too complicated to be understood by a mainstream audience.

There has been a lot of debate as to whether such a thing as *AI* can really exist. After all, most forms of AI and machine learning require some form of human input to get started and, so in that sense, they do not truly teach themselves. For example, Google's AlphaGo bot was able to beat the world's best Go player in a feat that people had previously thought was impossible. But even then, it did that by analyzing a huge database of existing games and drawing conclusions from the results. It is now one step closer to true AI as the researchers were able to tweak the software so that it taught itself entirely from scratch by playing games against itself and learning over time how to act more strategically. And, while this might seem at first as though it has little to do with healthcare, *The Guardian* reports that, "At DeepMind, which is based in London, AlphaGo Zero is working out how proteins fold, a massive scientific challenge that could give drug discovery a sorely needed shot in the arm." It will be interesting to see whether it succeeds.

Healthcare Applications

The idea behind bringing machine learning into the field of healthcare is that it can help to power much more advanced analytical systems that provide real-time insights.

Ed Corbett MD, Deputy Chief Medical Officer at Health Catalyst, explains:

Having easy access to the blood pressure and other vital signs when I see my patient is routine and expected. Imagine how much more useful it would be if I was also shown my patient's risk for stroke, coronary artery disease, and kidney failure based on the last 50 blood pressure readings, lab test results, race, gender, family history, socioeconomic status, and latest clinical trial data. We need to advance more information to clinicians so they can make better decisions about patient diagnoses and treatment options, while understanding the possible outcomes and cost for each one.[3]

Machine learning is at its most powerful when it is being applied to huge amounts of data that no human being could ever hope to process. There is a misconception in the healthcare industry that machine learning is some futuristic new concept that has no tangible applications, but the truth is that we are already starting to benefit from the insights that it has to offer. The key is to focus on finding specific ways that machine learning can be used across all different areas of the healthcare industry.

Of course, if you do not have access to the data, then you cannot process it, and our current electronic health record (EHR) systems are not interoperable and, therefore, reduce the amount of data that any one algorithm can have access to. The good news is that this opens up an opportunity for smaller companies to merge their data with larger ones. "At some point," Corbett says, "we may see regional data hubs with datasets customized for geographical, environmental and socioeconomic factors, that give healthcare systems of all sizes access to more data."

Corbett also refers to a presentation that he gave on the future of analytics and its impact on clinical care. "In my slides," he says, "I showed a hypothetical EMR running predictive algorithms while a doctor was examining his patient. A pop-up box displayed the real-time diagnosis, pathology results and treatment options, as well as each option's potential effectiveness and cost for this patient." While the patient in this case may have been hypothetical, it was modeled after his father who passed away several years ago from prostate cancer. He chose the scenario to demonstrate outcomes that could have been possible, had machine learning been available at the time. I have successfully built and implemented similar algorithms for heart failure and multiple sclerosis.

---

[3] See: http://bit.ly/machinelearninghealthcare

Corbett's father was given two years to live by his doctor, based upon what the physician knew about similar patients and the treatment options that were available. "My dad had a great oncologist," Corbett said, "but he was caring for thousands of patients with many different kinds of cancer. He could never have put in the time and effort needed to learn all the new drugs and treatment options coming out for all these cancers."

But, Corbett could. He spent time researching clinical trials and new treatment options, identifying which treatments were keeping people alive for longer and whether there were any unpleasant side effects. "Many times, I presented treatment options and clinical trials that my dad's doctor wasn't aware of," he explains.

> With my years of training and expertise, I could cull the literature and recommend the best options for my dad. In other words, I was the human algorithm, the doctor's brain who had the means and, most importantly, the motivation and time, to work in concert with my dad's physician to develop the optimal plan, which ultimately extended Dad's life nine years.

Of course, not all of us are lucky enough to have a physician in the family, but that is where AI comes in. Like Corbett says, he was acting as a human algorithm. Machine learning and its sister technology, natural language processing, could be exactly what we need to follow Corbett's approach for every single patient. And let us face it—who of us would not want to live an extra seven years if it had no detrimental impact on our quality of life?

Machine Learning for Breast Cancer

Mammograms are still the best available tests for breast cancer, but that has not stopped researchers from using AI and machine learning to improve early breast cancer detection. Manisha Bahl of Massachusetts General Hospital's Breast Imaging Fellowship Program has teamed up with MIT professor Regina Barzilay and Harvard professor Constance Lehman to drastically improve the way we treat breast cancer.

FashNerd explains that the system:

> uses machine learning to predict if a high-risk lesion identified on a needle biopsy after a mammogram will upgrade to cancer at surgery. When the process was tested on 335 high-risk lesions, the model correctly diagnosed 97% of the breast cancers as malignant and reduced the number of benign surgeries by more than 30% compared to existing approaches.[4]

This is good news for the one in eight women who will be diagnosed with breast cancer at some point during their lifetime. That is because the new technology could stop people from having to go for painful and invasive surgeries if they are not necessary. Barzilay, who is MIT's Delta Electronics Professor of Electrical Engineering and Computer Science, explained, "Because diagnostic tools are so inexact, there's an understandable tendency for doctors to over-screen for breast cancer. When there's this much uncertainty in data, machine learning is exactly the tool that we need to improve detection and prevent over-treatment."

Most exciting of all is that the model could be repurposed and applied to other types of cancer and even other diseases entirely, and the team is continuing to make improvements. Definitely one to watch.

The Human Side

I recently came across an insightful article by Benjamin Rogojan in which he investigated the problems with machine learning in the healthcare industry. What is interesting about this article in particular is that Rogojan is not a doctor or even a researcher at a big pharma company. He is a data engineer who just happens to work in the healthcare industry.

"[It's] both exciting and terrifying," Rogojan explains.

> In the past year and a half, I have spent my time developing several products to help healthcare professionals make better decisions. Specifically, I've been targeting healthcare quality, fraud and drug

---

[4]   See: http://bit.ly/mitaiarticle

misuse. As I was working on the various metrics and algorithms, I was constantly asking myself a few questions. How will this influence the patient's treatment? How will it influence the doctor's decision? Will this improve the long-term health of a population?[5]

Rogojan explains that most hospitals are run like businesses, but he also points out that their goal is not always just to boost their bottom lines. I believe that this is a view that is also held by some physicians, as well as their patients. He also points out that these decisions will have impact on the algorithms themselves. "The algorithms and models we build can't just be focused on the bottom line," Rogojan says. "Instead, we really need to take a moment to consider how they'll impact the patient and how metrics could change the behavior of a doctor in a way that might be negative."

Rogojan also highlights some other interesting challenges such as the issue of what happens when doctors over-adjust or over-compensate, correcting their behavior by too much and ending up doing more harm than good. For example, they might try to avoid being flagged as wasteful and end up not providing patients with sufficient amounts of medication.

"Could we possibly cause doctors to miss out on obvious diagnoses because they're so concerned about costing the hospital and patients too much money?" Rogojan wonders.

Or worse, perhaps they rely too strongly on their models to diagnose for them in the future. I know that I've over-adjusted my behavior in the past when I was provided with criticism, so what's to stop a doctor from doing the same? There's a fine line somewhere between allowing a human to make a good decision and forcing them to rely on the thinking of a machine.

It seems that he has also put some thought into the ethics behind his own profession. "There's a risk that we'll focus more on the numbers and less on what the patients are actually saying," Rogojan explains.

---

[5] See: http://bit.ly/rogojanmachinelearning

Doctors focusing too much on the numbers and not on the patient is a personal concern of mine. If a model is wrong for a company that's selling dress shirts or toasters, that means missing out on a sale and missing a quarterly goal. A model being wrong in healthcare could mean that someone dies or that they're not properly treated. So as flashy as it can be to create systems that help us to better make decisions, I do often wonder if we as humans have the discipline to not rely on them for the final say.

This Century's Penicillin

Award-winning technology journalist Oliver Pickup recently described machine learning as *this century's penicillin*, pointing to its applications in life-saving healthcare situations.[6] He points out that around a third of all human deaths around the world are caused by cardiovascular disease (CVD) and suggests that machine learning could be the solution that we need.

"It enables much speedier and more accurate diagnostic processes," Pickup explains. "It's already proving to be life-saving in healthcare in general and for those with CVD specifically, as related conditions can be identified early and impending strokes and heart attacks can be spotted in advance."

But it is not Pickup who coined the comparison to penicillin. That honor falls to Dr. Mitesh Patel, the U.K. medical director of health insurers Aetna International, who said:

The impact of machine learning will be as transformational to modern medicine as the discovery of penicillin was in the last century. [It] has the ability to spot signs of disease sooner than a clinician by comparing more complicated datasets and by reading heart scans at a lower error rate. It will read scans more quickly with more accuracy and allow physicians to support patients by alleviating their workload. Looking ahead, machine-learning will enable low-cost diagnostics to be widely available, providing greater support than ever before.

---

[6] See: http://bit.ly/thiscenturyspenicillin

Machine learning could also come in useful when it comes to helping us to manage our aging populations. Dr. Ronak Rajani, a cardiologist at the Harley Street Clinic, says:

Life expectancy in Britain is anticipated to increase to 85 years for a woman and 83 years for a man by 2030. If we plot the leading cause of mortality across varying decades, after the age of 50, cardiovascular disease is top and continues to rise with each decade of life. Unsurprisingly, CVD is one of the leading costs to healthcare systems in developed countries. Indeed, it's estimated that by 2030 the cost of CVD alone for governments will far exceed that of the annual military defense budget.

The biggest benefit of machine learning is its ability to process huge amounts of information. With CVD, for example, Dr. Rajani says:

The problem is that it's too vast, complex and heterogeneous, and [that it] changes too quickly for it to be used effectively by humans. The brain of a radiologist reporting eight cardiac computed tomography scans in an afternoon must process in excess of 650 million voxels of data, and it will need to provide an accurate diagnosis and opinion based on the latest evidence.

Another great example of machine learning's potential comes to us from Birmingham in the United Kingdom. Dr. Rahul Potluri, clinical lecturer in cardiology at the city's Aston Medical School, expects a widespread rollout of heart-tracking sensors "due to the development of the feature on the Apple Watch and other such devices." He also notes that machine learning could "potentially [have] the ability to monitor heart rhythms remotely in real time," which would "certainly [be] likely to improve diagnosis."

This is already happening to a certain extent at Birmingham's Children's Hospital, thanks to a team led by Heather Duncan. They have pioneered a study called RAPID (*Real-time Adaptive and Predictive Indicator of Deterioration*), which is the first of its kind in the world and which is based on McLaren's Formula 1 telemetry. "The most recent version of

RAPID can give us 10 hours' warning [before a cardiac arrest]," Duncan says, "rather than the four hours using routine methods. I'm very excited because I believe that soon all patients will be monitored wirelessly, and machine-learning and smart alarms are the future."

More Machine Learning Applications

Still not convinced about machine learning and its potential applications in the healthcare industry? I am willing to bet that within 3–5 years of this book's publication, machine learning in healthcare will be so widespread that the average person on the street will at least be familiar with the basic concepts. They will have heard about it on the news.

In a recent article on Medium,[7] Sciforce talked about machine learning and AI and their potential impact on the healthcare industry, highlighting eight main ways that they will come together to drive innovation:

Disease Identification and Diagnosis

With so many different diseases and so many new medical studies being published on a daily basis, it is impossible for a human doctor to know everything. The idea here is for machine learning systems to process all of this information and to distill it into actionable insights that we can put to use.

Personalized Treatment

The closest we currently have to true personalized treatment systems are supervised learning systems that allow physicians to choose from a limited pool of diagnoses and to estimate the patient's likelihood of having any given diagnoses. As these systems get better and better at what they do, it is likely that our reliance on them will continue to increase.

---

[7] See: http://bit.ly/sciforcemachinelearning

Smart Electronic Health Records

It is no secret that we need help with our EHRs. Machine learning could help to power optical character recognition (OCR) and natural language processing systems that allow computers to take on some of the filing while our physicians spend more time with patients.

Behavioral Modification

As our smartphones grow more powerful and new wearable devices and bio-sensors are created and adopted, we will create more and more data about our health and our lifestyles. This opens up the opportunity for us to receive real-time feedback to monitor the response to medical treatments and even to help us to modify our behaviors to avoid becoming ill in the first place.

Drug Discovery

Machine learning is already being touted as one of the most important tools when it comes to early-stage drug discovery, whether that is by screening drug compounds or whether it is by predicting success rates and helping to guide the directions that the research takes.

Clinical Trial Research

In a similar vein to its potential use for drug discovery, machine learning could help with clinical trials by crunching the numbers and analyzing the data. This could mean helping to process the results, but it could also mean helping to identify the best candidates for trials and even highlighting potential problem areas.

Epidemic Outbreak Prediction

Disease and epidemic outbreaks can pose huge threats to our populations, which is why we are increasingly turning to machine learning and AI to help us to predict them. If we can predict potential outbreaks, we can take steps to try to stop them and to make sure that we have appropriate medication and resources on hand to deal with them.

CHAPTER 4

Natural Language Processing in Healthcare

Chat bots represent the next evolution in natural language processing. And they provide a cheap and effective way to answer simple questions and provide a 24/7 access point between businesses and customers. Time to embrace our robot overlords.

—Casey Markee

Natural language processing (NLP) is pretty much exactly what it sounds like. It is an umbrella term that is used to refer to the ability of machines to process and understand language as it is written or spoken by human beings. While it would be nice to think that our languages make logical sense and follow basic rules of grammar and punctuation, we all know that is not always the case. We use slang, proper nouns, abbreviations, and acronyms, and not everyone can string a sentence together like Stephen King or J. K. Rowling.

That is where NLP comes in. Loosely speaking, it is a form of artificial intelligence (AI) that is all about trying to analyze and understand either written or spoken language and the context that it is being used in. A basic example of NLP in action is the predictive text that we see when we use our smartphones. As we type our messages, the phone's operating system uses AI and NLP to try to guess at what we might be typing and which words might come next.

NLP is not perfect, as you will have seen if you have ever used a tool like Google Translate, but it is pretty powerful and getting better all the time. It can even be combined with machine learning to create a system that can not only understand what is being said, but which will also continue to improve the more it is used. A great example here is Google Assistant, which gets better at understanding and responding to the commands of individual users. This can come in useful if you have an accent or a speech impediment, and it is all made possible by a combination of NLP and machine learning.

NLP is what makes chat bots possible. After all, they need to be able to take natural language as an input and then to use it again as an output. This is no small task, especially when it comes to the sheer number of possible permutations that are available when it comes to the way that we use language.

Still, today's programmers have risen to the challenge, which is why recent figures show that healthcare chat bot interactions are set to reach 2.8 billion by 2023.[1] According to IoT Global Network, a switch to using AI and chat bots will help the healthcare industry to save four billion U.S. dollars by 2023. It also found that chat bot adoption will increase because of a variety of factors, including patients becoming more comfortable with using them, shortages of medical practitioners, aging populations, and the increased sophistication of the software itself.

Natural Language Processing

Not many people are brave enough to tackle the complicated topic of NLP, but Dr. Robert Wachter has given it a good go. In an article for The Hospital Leader (the official blog for the Society of Hospital Medicine), Wachter shared an amazing description of NLP and the history of doctor note-taking, which I will do my best to summarize, but which I recommend checking out in its entirety if you get the time.[2]

Wachter argues that the ability for software to *read* notes could be one of the most important breakthroughs in digital medicine. He says, "A recent study linked the use of proton pump inhibitors to subsequent heart attacks. It did this by plowing through 16 million notes in electronic health records."

Back at the dawn of medicine in the time of Hippocrates, medical records were written in prose by the physician. Wachter cites medical historian Stanley Reiser, who describes the case of Apollonius of Abdera,

---

[1] See: http://bit.ly/healthcarebots2023
[2] See: http://bit.ly/wachternlp

who lived in the 5th century BCE. His doctor's note survived the test of time and reads,

> There were exacerbations of the fever; the bowels passed practically nothing of the food taken; the urine was thin and scanty. No sleep… About the fourteenth day from his taking to bed, after a rigor, he grew hot; wildly delirious, shouting, distress, much rambling, followed by calm; the coma came on at this time.[3]

Unfortunately, this story does not have a happy ending. The final entry in Apollonius of Abdera's medical record read, "34 day. Death."

Of course, medical health records have changed a lot since then. As we learned more about the human body, we were able to add more data points such as the results of blood tests and the stability of vital signs. Wachter explains that this was all well and good, until two major forces took root. The first was the change in audience for the doctor's note, which was suddenly of interest to a huge number of stakeholders, including "government officials, regulators, accreditors, payers, quality measurers and malpractice attorneys."

The second, Wachter says, was the digital transformation of medicine.

> Now, all the parties with a keen interest in the physician's note no longer had to sift through illegible scrawl. Fine. But they really wanted to know a limited set of facts, which could most efficiently be inventoried by forcing the doctor to fill in various templates and check dozens of boxes. This, of course, became an instant source of conflict, since physicians continue to be trained and socialized to think in stories. But the payer wants to know if the doctor recorded at least nine reviews of system elements. The quality measurer wants to know if the doctor documented smoking cessation counseling. And so on.

This is why, physicians are spending so much time filling out paperwork instead of speaking to their patients. This is also why modern patient

---

[3]   See: http://bit.ly/apolloniusrecord

records and doctor's notes are often so bloated and unintelligible that they have no practical use when it comes to helping patients.

And, it is where NLP comes in.

NLP is basically the ability of a computer program to understand human language, whether it is in the written or the spoken form. The idea is that if NLP software can understand the words in a doctor's note, it can fill out the forms on the doctor's behalf.

There are obstacles to overcome along the way, of course, and Wachter goes into more detail in his article for those who want to know more. Instead, I would like to leave you with the author's vision of the future:

> Think about a world in which a patient's electronic notes, going back many years, can be mined for key risk factors or other historical elements, without the need to constrain the search to structured data fields like prescription lists or billing records. Computers have wrenched us out of our world of narrative notes and placed us into an increasingly regimented, dehumanized world of templates and checklists. Wouldn't it be lovely if computers could liberate us from the checkboxes, allowing us to get back to the business of talking to our patients and describing their findings, and our thinking, in prose?

Natural Language Generation

One of the most exciting applications of AI is the potential for natural language generation (NLG). We are talking about AI being used to create written work, whether we are talking about news articles or whether we are talking about e-mails and social media updates.

Chicago's Narrative Science is at the forefront of this trend, thanks to a combination of timing, funding, and recognition. Founded back in 2010, the company has gone from strength to strength, raising 30 million U.S. dollars in funding and earning a spot on CB Insights' Artificial Intelligence 100 list. Their AI-created copy has even been published in *Forbes*.

But, what is interesting about Narrative Science and other companies that are working in this area is the fact that they are effectively providing the opposite of NLP, which allows AI to understand written and spoken language. The company's CEO, Stuart Frankel, explained,

> Advanced NLG platforms start by understanding what the user wants to communicate. Then these systems perform the relevant analysis to highlight what's most interesting and important, to identify and access the data necessary to tell the story, and finally to deliver the analysis in a personalized, easy-to-consume way: as a narrative.[4]

Of course, many of the products that are out on the market at the moment are focusing largely on automating time-consuming tasks like weather and finance reports, which follow a pre-defined formula. It will be much more difficult to create AI that can write creatively, and authors are unlikely to be replaced any time soon—which is good news for me!

Still, it is pretty easy to see the potential applications of NLG in the healthcare industry. We all know that physicians are spending far too much time filling out electronic medical records (EMRs), so why should we not outsource that work to an AI?

AIs could even be coming to take over in other creative areas, as is the case with NVidia's AI that creates *convincingly fake videos*, such as by taking a video of a snow-filled drive in the winter and turning it into summer.[5] It is done more convincingly than any human being could manage while simultaneously taking up much less manpower.

NLP in Healthcare

NLP has all sorts of applications across the board, from improving the completeness and accuracy of our medical health records to taking the written word and turning it into data that can be read by machines. It could even allow physicians to dictate their notes instead of having to sit in front of a computer to manually enter all of the data.

---

[4] See: http://bit.ly/narrativesciencenanalyze
[5] See: http://bit.ly/nvidianewai

A great example of the power of NLP and machine learning comes to us from IBM's Watson. The team at IBM partnered with EHR providers Epic and Virginia's Carillion Clinic to look at how NLP and machine learning could help to identify patients with heart disease. "Using unstructured data was found to be important in this project," IBM's Paul Hake explained.

> When physicians are recording information, they'll just prefer to type everything in one place into the notes section of the EMR. And so this information is kind of lost. It's then almost a manual process to map this unstructured information back into the EMR system so that we can use it for analytics.[6]

According to Jennifer Bresnick, Director of Editorial at Health IT Analytics,

> The pilot program successfully identified 8,500 patients who were at risk of developing congestive heart failure within the year. Watson ran through a whopping 21 million records in just six short weeks, and achieved an 85% accuracy rate for patient identification.

Vanessa Michelini, Distinguished Engineer and Master Inventor at IBM Watson Health, added,

> There's this explosion of data – not just genomic data, but all sorts of data – in the healthcare space, and the industry needs to find the best ways to extract what's relevant and to bring it together to help clinicians make the best decisions for their patients.

Bresnik notes that in 2014 alone, over 140,000 academic articles were published on the detection and treatment of cancer. Nobody could ever hope to read all of those studies and to distil them into actionable insights. That is where NLP and AI come in, and the two technologies are already being embedded into EHR systems.

That does not mean that adopting NLP is easy, though. "Unstructured clinical notes and narrative text still present a major problem for

---

[6]   See: http://bit.ly/nlpinhealthcare

computer scientists," Bresnick says. "True reliability and accuracy are still in the works, and certain problems such as word disambiguation and fragmented 'doctor speak' can stump even the smartest NLP algorithms."

"[Clinical text] is often ungrammatical," adds Hilary Townsend, MSI, in the *Journal of AHIMA*. "Clinical notes make heavy use of acronyms and abbreviations, making them highly ambiguous." As if that was not confusing enough, as much as a third of clinical abbreviations in the Unified Medical Language System (UMLS) Metathesaurus have multiple meanings, while more than half of terms that are typically used in clinical notes can be ambiguous. "For example, 'discharge' can signify either bodily excretion or release from a hospital," Townsend says.

As human beings, we naturally draw inferences from the context in which the words are being used. The idea is for NLP to do the same, although there is a long way to go until NLP can process language as well as a human being can. Still, we are heading in the right direction, and Allied Market Research predicts that the cognitive computing market will be worth 13.7 billion U.S. dollars by 2020, representing a 33.1% compound annual growth. They also project that 6.5 billion U.S. dollars will be spent on text analytics by 2020.

"Eventually," Bresnik concludes,

> natural language processing tools may be able to bridge the gap between the unfathomable amount of data generated on a daily basis and the limited cognitive capacity of the human mind. From the most cutting-edge precision medicine applications to the simple task of coding a claim for billing and reimbursement, NLP has nearly limitless potential to turn electronic health records from burden to boon.

The Three Types of NLP

According to a report from Chilmark Research, there are 12 main use cases for NLP in the healthcare industry, and they can be divided into three main categories.[7]

---

[7] See: http://bit.ly/beckershospitalchilmark

Mainstay NLP

NLP tools with a proven return on investment such as speech recognition, clinical documentation improvement, data mining research, computer-assisted coding, and automated registry reporting.

Emerging NLP

NLP tools that are likely to have an immediate impact such as clinical trial matching, prior authorization, clinical decision support, and risk adjustment and hierarchical condition categories.

Next-Generation NLP

NLP tools that are on the horizon such as ambient virtual scribes, population surveillance, computational phenotyping, and biomarker discovery.

The full report, titled *Natural Language Processing: Unlocking the Potential of a Digital Healthcare Era*, explains,

> The current market for natural language processing (NLP) technology in healthcare is nascent, dominated by a few legacy vendors that are focusing on front-end speech recognition (for computer-assisted physician documentation) and back-end coding (to optimize billing). While many vendors continue to advance NLP technology for more general use, there are a handful of niche solutions from highly specialized healthcare vendors pursuing additional opportunities to apply the technology. The research delves into a dozen such notable applications, including computer-assisted coding, speech recognition and data mining.[8]

Examples of NLP

The beauty of NLP is that when you are using it, you rarely know that it is there. Like AI, it is used under the hood to power software, processing the inputs and the outputs without the explicit knowledge of the user.

---

[8]   See: http://bit.ly/chilmarkmlpreport

That does not mean that there is a shortage of examples to highlight the technology's potential, though. Here are a few of my favorites.

Veterans Affairs

The U.S. Department of Veterans Affairs used NLP to scan over two billion EHRs to identify any indications of post-traumatic stress disorder (PTSD), depression, or self-harm among veteran patients with an 80 percent accuracy rate.

MIT Research

Researchers at the Massachusetts Institute of Technology achieved a 75 percent accuracy rate when using NLP to decipher the semantic meaning of clinical terms by using a statistical probability model to identify the context.

Schizophrenia

By analyzing the speech patterns of patients with schizophrenia, NLP achieved a 100 percent accuracy rate at identifying which patients were likely to experience psychosis.

UCLA

By combining NLP with ICD-9 codes and lab data, researchers at the University of California, Los Angeles (UCLA) were able to identify patients with cirrhosis.

University of Alabama

Researchers at the university used NLP to identify cancer at a rate that was 22.6 percent more accurate than the manual review of medical records.

We already know that NLP is the perfect tool to understand written and spoken language and to convert it to a consistent format that can be understood by machines and human beings alike. Just a few of the most common use cases for NLP include:

> **#1:** Summarizing huge amounts of text (such as from published medical articles in reputable journals) so that only the most relevant information is displayed.

#2: Improving the integrity of clinical data by converting unstructured text into standardized information that can easily be read and understood by machines.

#3: Converting data from machine-readable information into easy-to-understand natural language for reporting, education, and other purposes.

#4: Synthesizing data from multiple sources to answer complex queries.

#5: Using optical character recognition (OCR) to turn images (such as PDF files or scans of physical documents) into text files that can be edited, parsed, and analyzed.

#6: Using speech recognition to allow physicians to dictate their notes and to carry out voice searches.

Voice Applications

"Hey Google, what is natural language processing?"

Okay, perhaps, you own an Alexa or you prefer to turn to Siri, but the idea is the same. Whenever you interact with a voice-based application such as a personal assistant, you are seeing NLP in action. It makes sense, when you think about it: we talk in *natural language*, and our home hub devices take that input and process it before determining the most appropriate response.

The great thing about voice applications is that they are able to change the way that we look at work. They are particularly useful in situations where we need to access information while going hands-free, which is why the adverts often show people cooking or driving. In a healthcare situation, it is easy to see how voice recognition technology could help surgeons while they are in the operating theater. A virtual assistant could provide responses to questions about the patient's medical information, adjust the lighting, take notes, or even just change the music that the surgery team is listening to.

I recently came across a piece by MobiHealthNews where they listed 37 different startups that are building voice applications for healthcare, separating them into different categories and showing how they intersect.

"As the next frontier in human-technology interfaces," they explain, voice-enabled and voice-first technologies are leading the way in many innovative applications across industries. Predictions that 50% of searches will be voice-based by 2020 and that 55% of US households will have a smart speaker by 2022 have entrepreneurs, developers, product managers and marketers rushing to figure out how they can capture the upcoming surge of voice-based technology. In healthcare, voice technology finds a market particularly ripe with potential and impactful use cases. The high cost of labor for physicians and other skilled workers – who spent countless hours inputting data into their electronic health records – is one example of an opportunity for startups to disrupt the status quo. In fact, one landscape of B2B voice technology startups across all verticals found that 47.1% of companies that were focused on a single sector were focused on healthcare.[9]

This makes healthcare the single biggest sector for developers of specialist voice technology apps, so perhaps it is no surprise that MobiHealth-News was able to create such a comprehensive list of different startups in the industry. Here is how those startups break down by category:

Aging in Place

Cuida Health, ElliQ, LifePod, Memory Lane, Reminder Rosie, Remind-MeCare, and Senter.

Patient-Provider Communication

Aiva, Merit.ai, Praktice.ai, Syllable, and VoiceFriend.

Physician Notes

Kiroku, MDOps, Notable, Saykara, Sopris Health, Suki, and Tenor.ai.

Speech and Hearing Difficulty

Ava, VocaliD, and Voiceitt.

---

[9] See: http://bit.ly/voiceappshealthcare

Development Platforms

ConversationHealth and Orbita.

Vocal Biomarkers

BeyondVerbal, Cogito, Corti, Healthymize, NeuroLex, Sonde, and WinterLight Labs.

Patient Engagement

CardioCube, CareAngel, HealthTap, Sensely, Kencor Health, and Pillo.

The Challenges of NLP

In order for us to make the most of NLP, we first need to understand the challenges that we will face and what is stopping us from using the technology to its full potential. The interesting thing here is that while healthcare executives need to understand this, so too do the engineers who will design the NLP systems that will help to cut costs and boost efficiencies across the healthcare industry.

According to Mike Dow, technical director at Health Catalyst,

> NLP requires that data engineers transform unstructured text into a usable format and in a location where the NLP technology can make use of it. This NLP pre-requisite can be a complex process, involving larger data sets and different technologies than many data engineers are familiar with.[10]

According to Dow, the four biggest challenges of working with NLP are:

More Volume

An average EMR record runs to around 100 bytes, or 100 MB per million records. The problem is that the average clinical note record is 150 times bigger. This is fine for smaller systems, but it can cause problems with larger systems that process millions or tens of millions of records.

---

[10]   See: http://bit.ly/nlpchallenges

Disparate Data Sources

This all comes back to the problem of decentralization in the healthcare industry. Because different EMR vendors use different data formats and different industry standards, it often means that the records are incompatible. This is challenging enough when it comes to binary information (i.e., *yes/no* fields), but it is even more difficult when it comes to unstructured data in free text fields (i.e., a physician's written notes on their patient).

Scattered Data

Dow says, "Clinical notes, radiology reports and pathology reports may exist in two or three different sets of tables, depending on the source system." When data is stored in different systems, it can be difficult to access it and almost impossible to update it. This is one of the biggest problems with our current medical records system and is the reason why people end up with multiple medical records after visiting different providers.

Understanding Documentation

This means getting to know how people are documenting patient data out in the real world, instead of just assuming that they will follow best practices. "For example," Dow says,

> during a recent project to identify adverse events for patients, we searched for documentation of in-hospital falls. The patient safety expert I was working with, a nurse, had always seen patient falls documented in nursing progress notes, but we found very few mentions of any falls in those notes. After discussions with the health information management group and nurses at the health system, we learned that it used a structured-only documentation methodology for nursing, and the best source for documentation of in-hospital falls would be the physician progress notes. This insight made a small difference in how our data scientist searches for falls data, but it made a significant difference in the results.

CHAPTER 5

Robotics in Healthcare

There are an endless number of things to discover about robotics. A lot of it is just too fantastic for people to believe.

—Daniel H. Wilson

When we think about robotics, it is easy for us to picture the kind of high-tech juggernauts that we are familiar with from sci-fi movies and video games. Either that or we think about creepy, all-too-human robots that freak people out because of the uncanny valley, the phenomenon that occurs when robots look similar to human beings, but which fail to be fully realistic. It can lead to an unsettling feeling that puts people on edge.

The good news is that the uncanny valley only applies when robots are trying and failing to accurately imitate humans, and most of the robots used in the healthcare profession are designed with a specific purpose in mind. There is no need to waste time and resources trying to make a robot look like a human being when you are using it for healthcare purposes.

In fact, the robotics used in the healthcare industry are drastically different from the popular perception of what a robot should look like, and you should go into this chapter without any of your preconceived notions about what a robot actually is. Let us take a look at what robots look like when it comes to healthcare.

Biopsies and Eye Operations

This is probably one of the coolest, most science fiction-inspired pieces of technology that I have seen in recent years, but that does not make it any less practical or impressive.

According to Mashable, a team at the University of Twente is working on *an MRI-compatible, biopsy-performing robot* called the Stormram

4, which could improve cancer screenings by performing biopsies.[1] The device is 3D printed, which means it is unaffected by the magnets inside an MRI machine, and it is driven by air pressure motors that allow accurate needle control to take tissue samples from a precise area.

The research and development is still at an early stage, but if the technology hits the mainstream, then it should help to ensure quicker and more accurate breast cancer diagnoses, saving lives and improving outlooks.

Robots have already been used to carry out prostate surgery and gallbladder procedures, but Futurism recently reported on an even more precise piece of surgery in which a robot operated on a human eye. "A surgeon uses a joystick to control the mobile arm of the PRECEYES system," writer Kristin Houser explains.[2] "Doctors can attach various instruments to the arm, and because the system is robotic, it does not suffer from any of the slight tremors that plague even the most steady-handed of humans."

To trial the device, surgeons performed operations on 12 similar patients and used the robot for half of them while treating the others in the traditional way. "All 12 surgeries were successful," Houser says.

In some cases, the robot made the surgeon even more effective than usual. In a second phase of the trial, surgeons used the robot on three patients to dissolve under-retina hemorrhages that could have led to vision loss. Those surgeries were successful, too. [The] robot-assisted eye surgery did take about three times as long as a traditional one, but trial leader Robert MacLaren told New Scientist that was just because the surgeons were unfamiliar with the robot and moved slowly out of caution.

Why Robots and Healthcare Go Together

Robots have a lot of advantages over mere mortals. For example, they do not get sick or tired, they do not need to take breaks to eat and while

---

[1] See: http://bit.ly/3dprintedmri

[2] See: http://bit.ly/roboteyeop

they are not invulnerable, they are at least less likely to fall victim to the inherent biases that we have as human beings.

In an article for his website, Dr. Bertalan Meskó, The Medical Futurist, listed some of the key uses of robotics in healthcare,[3] including:

Surgical Precision

Machines can be much more accurate than a human could ever be, moving with such precision that you would need a microscope just to see it.

Blood Samples

Some robots can now take blood samples and carry out other basic tasks, freeing up physicians' time and allowing them to concentrate more on talking to and understanding the patient.

Robotic Assistance

Robots are increasingly being used to provide care and support to patients, especially among the elderly. This will become even more important as populations continue to age.

Exoskeletons

Once purely the domain of science fiction, exoskeletons are basically specialized devices to increase the capability of a human being's body. They can be used to help with rehabilitation and even to allow paralyzed people to return to work, and they could also one day be used to help nurses to reduce the strain that comes from lifting and moving patients.

Supply Chain

Robots are being used across all sorts of different industries as part of the supply chain to automate production or to take on tasks that are too dangerous for human beings to do. Ultimately, it brings down the cost

---

[3] See: http://bit.ly/roboticshealthcare

of production and could help to save the healthcare system some much-needed money.

Microrobotics

Not all robots are big, hulking machines. We are increasingly seeing smaller robots being developed for specialist use cases, such as being inserted into capsules and used to remove foreign objects from patients' stomachs.

Companion Robots

Nearly half of Americans feel lonely.[4] Companion robots could be one way to combat this, particularly in vulnerable people such as the disabled or those with mental health issues.

AI and Robotics

International consulting agency PwC recently released a report in which they highlighted eight of the main ways that artificial intelligence (AI) and robotics are transforming the way we look at healthcare. "AI is getting increasingly sophisticated at doing what humans do," the report explains, "but more efficiently, more quickly and at a lower cost. The potential for both AI and robotics is vast. Just like in our everyday lives, AI and robotics are increasingly a part of our healthcare ecosystem."[5]

Staying Well

Prevention is better than the cure. AI is able to crunch huge amounts of data to make bespoke recommendations to help healthy people to stay healthy.

Early Detection

AI is already faster and more accurate than human beings when it comes to diagnosing certain diseases. "The use of AI is enabling review and

---

4   See: http://on-ajc.com/lonelinessepidemicajc
5   See: http://pwc.to/aihealthcarepwc

translation of mammograms 30 times faster with 99% accuracy, reducing the need for unnecessary biopsies," the report explains.

Diagnosis

Building on from early detection, AI and robotics can also help with diagnostics. It could also provide a useful backstop, automatically reevaluating scans to make sure that human eyes have not missed anything.

Decision Making

AI-based tools could help physicians to make important treatment decisions based on the huge amounts of data that we create on a daily basis. "Using pattern recognition to identify patients at risk of developing a condition – or seeing it deteriorate due to lifestyle, environmental, genomic, or other factors – is another area where AI is beginning to take hold in healthcare," the report says.

Treatment

"Robots have been used in medicine for more than 30 years," PwC explains.

> They range from simple laboratory robots to highly complex surgical robots that can either aid a human surgeon or execute operations by themselves. In addition to surgery, they're used in hospitals and labs for repetitive tasks, in rehabilitation, physical therapy and in support of those with long-term conditions.

End-of-Life Care

Robots are already being used in a variety of situations to assist with end-of-life care, with the goal of allowing people to remain independent for longer and reducing the burden on hospitals and care homes. The report says, "AIs, combined with the advancements in humanoid design, are enabling robots to go even further and have 'conversations' and other social interactions with people to keep aging minds sharp."

Research

It takes an average of 12 years for a drug to go from research lab to the hands of patients, and only 0.1 percent of the drugs that go into preclinical testing make it to human testing. Even then, only one in five of those 0.1 percent are then approved for human usage. It costs an average of 2.6 billion U.S. dollars to develop a new drug and to get it into the hands of patients.[6] Fortunately for us—and for our cash-strapped healthcare industry—AI could help to direct research and to streamline the drug development process, cutting both development costs and time to market.

Training

AI does a great job of running complex simulations, and indeed, this is largely what the field of predictive analytics relies upon. AI is already being used to power simulations for the military, and it is only natural that it will also find its way into healthcare training. "The advent of natural speech and the ability of an AI computer to draw instantly on a large database of scenarios [are particularly important for the healthcare industry]," the report says. "And the training program can learn from the trainee, meaning that the challenges can be continually adjusted to meet their learning needs."

Robots and the UK's National Health Service

A 2018 report from the Institute for Public Policy Research (IPPR), carried out in conjunction with surgeon and ex-health minister Lord Darzi, investigated how robotics could be used within the National Health Service (NHS) to improve patient outcomes and to help the struggling healthcare industry to meet tougher deadlines with lower budgets.

According to Denis Campbell in *The Guardian*:

Robots could soon help hospital patients to eat their meals, diagnose serious illnesses and even help people to recover from operations, in an artificial intelligence revolution in the NHS. Machines

---

[6]   See: http://bit.ly/newdrugdevelopment

could take over a wide range of tasks currently done by doctors, nurses, healthcare assistants and administrative staff.[7]

The report found that adopting AI and embracing *full automation* could free up the equivalent of 12.5 billion pounds in staff time, allowing them to spend more time with their patients. The report explained, "Given the scale of productivity savings required in health and care – and the shortage of frontline staff – automation presents a significant opportunity to improve both the efficiency and the quality of care in the NHS."

The report points to technology like *bedside robots* that could help hospital patients to eat, drink, and move around the ward. They could potentially even help with post-surgical rehabilitation exercises. The report also suggests that new admissions to hospitals could first undergo "digital triage in an automated assessment suite" where "AI-based systems, including machine learning algorithms, would be used to make more accurate diagnoses of diseases such as pneumonia, breast and skin cancers, eye diseases and heart conditions."

It is interesting to note that the report echoes some of the other insights that I have included elsewhere in the book while discussing the potential of AI. It found that new technologies could take over patients' health records, as well as helping them to book appointments and to process prescriptions. It also concluded that AI will not lead to a loss of jobs—good news for the 1.3 million people who are employed by the NHS—and that machines would work alongside human beings instead of outright replacing them. If anything, AI could be the savior of the NHS. Andrew Foster, chief executive of the Wrightington, Wigan, and Leigh NHS trust and former director of human resources for the NHS, explained, "We currently have at least 100,000 vacancies in the NHS with demand rising all the time. I think that redundant NHS staff is a long way from being a significant concern."

However, he did also address concerns that the IPPR's vision might not be plausible. "It is realistic that significant elements of patient care could be improved by robotics and artificial intelligence," he explained.

---

[7] See: http://bit.ly/robotsinthenhs

However, we must never forget the fundamental importance of human care, compassion, empathy and even the importance of a gentle, physical, human touch. For it to be welcome, health services will have to sensitively blend new technologies with old-fashioned care.

In other words, humans and machines partnering for better outcomes.

The good news is that if the report is correct and AI can drive 12.5 billion pounds in efficiencies, it could be just what we need to keep the cash-strapped NHS going. "Information released by hospitals in England under freedom of information laws show widespread continued use of very old X-ray machines as well as CT, MRI and ultrasound scanners," *The Guardian* explains. The NHS is also the world's largest purchaser of fax machines,[8] although it was recently revealed that the organization had banned the purchase of new machines and that they would be phasing them out completely by March 31, 2020.[9]

Shadow health secretary Jonathan Ashworth sums up the dilemma that the NHS is facing by explaining, "Eight years of Tory austerity funding imposed on our NHS have led to a backlog of £5 billion of repairs to crumbling hospitals and old equipment that in some cases is decades past its sell-by date." He points to the fact that hospitals have often been unable to replace outdated equipment in recent years because the government used 3.8 billion pounds of NHS capital funding, "which pays for repairs, new buildings and new equipment," to cover hospital running costs.

So, while robotics and AI could potentially be the savior of the cash-strapped health agency, they could also be cost-prohibitive. It is a catch-22 that British politicians are likely to debate for the months and years to come, and it will be interesting to see what the end result is.

Robotics and Caregiving

I recently had the good fortune to come across an opinion piece by Louise Aronson in *The New York Times* in which she shared her vision of the future

---

[8]   See: http://bit.ly/nhsfaxmachines
[9]   See: http://ind.pn/faxmachineban

of robot caregivers. Aronson is an associate professor of geriatrics at the University of California, San Francisco, as well as the author of *A History of the Present Illness*, so you could say that she knows what she is talking about.

What strikes me about this article is that it was published back in July 2014, which is a long time ago when it comes to technological development. We have already made huge leaps and bounds in terms of the actual technology, but what Aronson nailed is the reason for using robotics in the first place. "Each time I make a house call," Aronson explains,

> I stay much longer than I should. I can't leave because my patient is holding my hand, or because she's telling me, not for the first time, about when Aunt Mabel cut off all her hair and they called her a boy at school, or how her daddy lost his job and the lights went out and her mother lit pine cones and danced and made everyone laugh. Sometimes I can't leave because she just has to show me one thing, but getting to that thing requires that she rise unsteadily from her chair, negotiate her walker through the narrow hallway, and find whatever it is in the dim light of her bedroom. I can, and do, write prescriptions for her many medical problems, but I have little to offer for the two conditions that dominate her days: loneliness and disability.

This is a great example of what the future of healthcare means to me. Technology alone is not going to solve problems, but it may help us to re-humanize the field and to take medicine back to its roots. And, ironically, robots might be the answer.

"In an ideal world," Aronson says,

> each of us would have at least one kind and fully capable human caregiver to meet our physical and emotional needs as we age. But most of us do not live in an ideal world, and a reliable robot may be better than an unreliable or abusive person, or than no one at all. Caregiving is hard work. More often than not, it is tedious, awkwardly intimate and physically and emotionally exhausting. Sometimes it is dangerous or disgusting. Almost always it is 24/7 and unpaid or low wage, and has profound adverse health consequences for those who do it.

Robots are already being used for a number of different use cases, and the United States of America risks falling behind, especially when compared to other developed nations like Japan. According to Aronson,

> The biggest argument for robot caregivers is that we need them. We do not have anywhere near enough human caregivers for the growing number of older Americans. Robots could help solve this workforce crisis by strategically supplementing human care. Equally important, robots could decrease high rates of neglect and abuse of older adults by assisting overwhelmed human caregivers and replacing those who are guilty of intentional negligence or mistreatment.

The Risks of Robotics

Robots are all well and good, but only when they work as they are supposed to. One interesting case was brought to my attention by NBC News after a series in which over 250 reporters in 36 countries investigated medical device alerts from across the globe. Here, Cynthia McFadden and Kevin Monahan report from Iowa, while Emily Siegel, Andrew W. Lehren, and Pauliina Siniauer report from New York City.[10]

Our story begins in Iowa, where Laurie Featherstone is about to have a hysterectomy. Just before the surgery was due to take place, she was asked a question she was not expecting: Would you like the surgeon to use a robot to carry out the procedure?

The robot in question was the da Vinci surgical system from Intuitive Surgical, and the doctor herself recommended it because it had less downtime, less scarring, and a complication rate of below 3 percent. It was also said to reduce recovery time, and so, Featherstone opted for the robot. Everything seemed to be going well… until a couple of weeks later, when complications started to make themselves apparent.

"Excess fluids accumulated in her kidneys," the authors explain.

---

[10] See: http://bit.ly/medicaldevicealerts

An ailment called hydronephrosis. There was an injury to one of her ureters, the duct that carries urine from the kidney to the bladder. One of her doctors wrote in her medical records that he assumed "the problem is a thermal injury" and was "due to robotic hysterectomy." Her ureter was burned and her colon damaged during the surgery, according to her medical records. Her prognosis calls for a permanent colostomy.

Featherstone initially filed a lawsuit against both Intuitive and her doctor's practice, but she later withdrew it after coming up against the statute of limitations. Her case is also an isolated one, and the da Vinci Surgical System is still heralded as a breakthrough. It has its advantages, but it also has its risks. That is what makes it such an ethical minefield.

Dr. Robert Poston, chief of cardiothoracic surgery at SUNY Downstate Medical Center, is a keen user of the device, but he does also warn that some surgeons start using it with insufficient training. "It's woefully inadequate, the way it's currently being done," Poston says.

We shouldn't be operating until we've done all of the training that we think is reasonable. We should live in a world where we practice brutal transparency with our patients. So if we lived in that world, we would tell the patient, "I'd like to operate on you but I didn't have the time or money to have all the training that I think I ought to have had. Is that okay?"

Poston says,

The root cause is the training. It's down to the willingness to sell robots to people and promote them doing surgeries when they aren't adequately trained, as well as the willingness of hospital credentialing committees to sign off on them and allow them to do it.

The Future of Healthcare Delivery

Recent research from PwC found that 54 percent of people in Europe, the Middle East, and Africa would be willing to engage with AI and robotics for healthcare, while up to 73 percent would be willing to undergo minor surgery at the hands of a robot.

Covering the revealing statistics and interviewing PwC's health industries consulting leader Brian Pomering, Health Europa explained,

> AI and robots will come to have a dramatic effect on the way we deliver and experience healthcare in the future. AI and robotics could make healthcare more accessible, treatment more affordable and diagnoses more accurate, but unlocking this potential will require a step-change in the way governments, health professionals, businesses and the public alike think about healthcare provision, and a significant number of obstacles will need to be overcome if the true power of technology is to be realized in practice.[11]

The PwC report is interesting because it highlights some unusual discrepancies. For example, talking about the willingness of patients to use AI and other new technologies, Pomering explains,

> [It depends] on which country you ask. We know that the UK is far more skeptical about using new technologies than countries in Africa or the Middle East, for example: just 39% of the people we surveyed in the UK said they were willing to use AI and robotics as part of their care compared to 94% in Nigeria and 85% in Turkey. At the macro-level, our research also found that people in Scotland and Wales are generally more willing to embrace the use of AI and robotics than those in England, which relates back to how easy it is to gain access to the healthcare service in your area and how long you have to wait for appointments.

It is a shame that those in the United Kingdom are less prepared to turn to AI and robotics because the National Health Service is under ever increasing pressure to do more with less. AI could be the solution that the NHS badly needs to reduce its expenditure and to increase the resources

---

[11] See: http://bit.ly/aihealthcaretransformation

it has available to offer treatments. On top of that, while patients in Nigeria and Turkey may be more prepared to put their trust in new technologies, it comes down to access. The United Kingdom leads the way in many areas of health technology, but if patients are unwilling to use that technology, then it reduces the impetus that the Brits have to keep on researching and may ultimately slow health-tech development across the globe.

"People in the UK like what they have," Pomering says.

Whereas in Nigeria, which we found to be the most willing to embrace AI and robotics, people's attitudes are very different. Over there, people understandably feel that being able to interact directly with a machine or a robot is better than not being able to interact with anything or anyone at all, and the clinicians, who are significantly overworked, see AI as a way of alleviating the pressures they're under and enabling them to achieve more. The more the NHS begins to come under pressures in this country, the more willing physicians and patients will become to embrace and engage with AI and robotics.

A Brief History of Healthcare Robots

Robotics is nothing new, but its mainstream adoption into the healthcare industry (beyond just the supply chain) is a relatively recent phenomenon. It is partly because healthcare is heavily regulated, and the ethical issues around having robots operating on humans have led to much hand-wringing and debate among healthcare staff. Still, there seems to be no doubt that robots and healthcare are a perfect match, especially when it comes to performing delicate operations that require a high level of accuracy.

The first robotic surgical assistant, the da Vinci Surgical System, was first approved by the Food and Drug Administration (FDA) and introduced into hospital settings back in 2000. Since then, it has helped to carry out over 20,000 surgical operations. Researchers at the Georgia Institute of Technology have even been able to give robots the sense of touch using artificial skin, a technological advance that has the potential to improve the quality of life of patients with disabilities.

"The ability of a robot to sense pressure is an important advancement in the ability of robots to deliver care to humans," Nadine Salmon explains in an article for RN.com. "Currently, artificial skin is being tested on a robotic arm using a series of sensors to transmit information to a computer that determines how much pressure the robot should exert when in contact with humans."

Salmon suggests that healthcare robots typically fall into one of two categories: those that replace jobs that were previously handled by humans and those that use telemedicine to connect physicians and patients in different locations. Other healthcare robots that she highlights include the Bestic Arm (which helps patients to eat their meals) and Toyota's Healthcare Assistants (which help with rehabilitation and aim to get people walking again). Then, there is Aethon's Tugs, a mobile robot that is used to transport medications, fresh linen, and laboratory results, as well as AIST's Paro, a robotic baby seal that is used for patients with dementia.

The Preliminary Visit of the Future

Every single one of us will experience a preliminary visit to a physician at some point in our lives. It is a fundamental part of the healthcare industry and the point at which we start looking for some sort of diagnosis. This process is already being changed by services like Forward, One Medical, Iora Health, and Push Doctor, which aim to ease the load on physicians by taking on some of their work and freeing up resources, but this is just the start.

This is illustrated perfectly by a recent piece on medical robotics for Analytics Insight, in which the authors explain,

> The preliminary clinical visit in the near future will be directed by a physical robot, molded like a human, who will find out about you before you begin talking. Your imperative signs like temperature, pulse, blood pressure and breathing rate will be estimated by the robotic clinician [using] infrared and retinal scan innovation, among different techniques still being developed. A couple of brisk moves and within seconds your new robotic friend will

know the constituents of your sweat, and thus your hydration
level and the status of certain organ capacities.[12]

The Analytics Insight piece also echoes my call for a more life-
style-based form of healthcare. As we create more and more data
through our wearable devices and our smartphones, we will have
greater insights than ever before on how our lifestyles are affecting our
bodies.

"We carry our smartphones everywhere we go." It is hard to measure exactly how much time we are spending on our mobile devices, but
most studies agree we spend around four hours per day interacting with
them.[13] When you compare that to the fact that the average doctor's visit
lasts around 15 minutes[14] and the average American visits the doctor four
times per year,[15] you arrive at a shocking statistic. It takes the average
American four years of doctors' visits to spend as much time with their
physician as they spend with their phone in a single day.

Robotics could be the perfect way to meet the ever-rising demand
for healthcare provision, especially as the world's population continues to
increase. "However," Analytics Insight cautions,

> let's not forget that there might be certain challenges to widely
> adopting medical robotics in the healthcare industries. Difficul-
> ties for robot-helped medical procedures will consist of increas-
> ing dimensions of independence, and additionally, the related
> legal and moral obstructions. Fortunately, we live in an ener-
> gizing era and can perceive a future that holds incredible guar-
> antees for pushing the limits of what's conceivable in medicinal
> services.

---

[12] See: http://bit.ly/analyticsinsightreport
[13] See: http://bit.ly/timespentonmobile
[14] See: http://bit.ly/averagevisitlength
[15] See: http://bit.ly/americandoctorvisits

More Healthcare Robots

Tech and healthcare are a match made in heaven, as *The Telegraph* proved while promoting its STEM Awards.[16] They pulled together a stunning list of robotics devices in the healthcare industry that highlights just how far these new technologies have come along. Here are just a few of the best:

The Da Vinci Surgical System

This surgical robot is controlled by a surgeon and mimics their hand and wrist movements, allowing them to treat more advanced conditions while reducing the risk of error.

Senhance

Developed by TransEnterix, this robotic assistant allows surgeons to control its arms while viewing a three-dimensional view of the operation. It also offers eye tracking and has recently been approved by the FDA.

Pepper

Brought to us by SoftBank Robotics, Pepper is said to be the world's first humanoid robot that is capable of recognizing human emotions. It can communicate using body movements and voice and has been used in retail, as well as in healthcare.

Robear

Created by Japanese firm RIKEN-SRK, Robear is a nursing care robot that aims to restore independence to the sick and the elderly. According to *The Telegraph*, "Robear is said to be strong enough to life patients out of bed, but also gentle enough to provide support as they sit down in wheelchairs."

---

[16]   See: http://bit.ly/stemhealthcare

Robotic Eye Surgery

Robots are at their best when they are performing specialized tasks. That is why, they appealed to Professor Robert MacLaren and his team at Oxford's John Radcliffe Hospital, where they successfully carried out the world's first robotic eye surgery. According to *The Telegraph*, "He used a remotely controlled robot to lift a membrane 1/100th of a millimeter thick from the retina at the back of [the patient's right eye]."

CHAPTER 6

Data in Healthcare

Data is a precious thing and will last longer than the systems themselves.
—*Tim Berners-Lee*

Data is the Holy Grail of healthcare. The more data we have, the more we can analyze it, learn from it, and use it to treat both individual patients and the population as a whole.

I am a big fan of Sherlock Holmes. The world's most famous consulting detective used the data he gathered in each of his investigations to arrive at a conclusion, and he was doing this as far back as 1887. We all create huge amounts of data on a daily basis, and yet, precious little makes it into our health records. Today's healthcare system, then, is much more Dr. Watson than Sherlock Holmes—and it is a Dr. Watson who is trying to theorize before he has data.

But, with data comes the problem of data ownership, as well as the legislative barriers that are put in place to make sure that data is stored and processed correctly. Strictly speaking, much of the data about patients is technically owned by the electronic health record (EHR) company, but that will not always be the case. Eric Topol MD recently sparked a Twitter debate about the whole situation in which he began his argument with a simple—but accurate—statement: "It's your body."[1]

This is reminiscent of an article by breast cancer survivor Stacey Tinianov in which she talks about how her healthcare records are scattered between different institutions. "There are even more health records of mine spread across the country," she wrote.

> Yet, with these "chapters" of my health behind various firewalls, the complete story is only in my head. The burden of tying the

---

[1] See: http://bit.ly/topolyourbody

highlights of my health history together for every new healthcare provider falls on my shoulders; a doable task, but certainly not an easy task in the typical 15-minute visit window.[2]

But, data has to come from somewhere, which is why, we are increasingly going to need new medical devices like the DiaMonTech no-invasive glucose monitoring device. The idea is to shift power back into the hands of patients so that they can monitor their own health as easily as possible. DiaMonTech's Markus Teuber explains,

> We've developed a technology called photo-thermal detection which emits light. This light penetrates your skin, where glucose molecules absorb it, and therefore you have tiny changes in temperature. These are detected by our device and can give you an accurate result on your glucose levels.[3]

Instead of relying on regular blood tests, which can be painful and detrimental to a patient's quality of life, patients with the DiaMonTech device can monitor their glucose levels around the clock and share that data with a healthcare provider.

The good news is that we have already started to create much of the healthcare data that we will need if we are to usher in the future. In fact, one report from the Stanford University School of Medicine concluded,

> The sheer volume of healthcare data is growing at an astronomical rate: 153 exabytes (one exabyte = one billion gigabytes) were produced in 2013 and an estimated 2,314 exabytes will be produced in 2020, translating to an overall rate of increase [of] at least 48% annually.[4]

Not bad.

---

[2] See: http://bit.ly/healthdatachapters
[3] See: http://bit.ly/diamontech
[4] See: http://stan.md/stanfordmedicinereport

Data Errors

The problem with our existing healthcare records is that they are not always right. In fact, one article by CNBC described medical record errors as *common* and *hard to fix*, citing the case of college student Morgan Gleason.[5]

Gleason was diagnosed with juvenile dermatomyositis nine years ago, and so, she is no stranger to the healthcare industry. In fact, she spends so much time interacting with the healthcare system that she goes out of her way to request a copy of her medical records after every visit. A couple of years ago, she paid a visit to a women's health clinic in Florida and discovered that her health record said she had given birth to two children, and that one of them had died. The only problem was that Gleason had never been pregnant.

To make matters worse, Gleason had also discovered a mistake in a different record, which falsely said that she had diabetes. She only became suspicious when her doctor started asking her questions about her blood sugar levels.

According to academic Ross Koppel, 70 percent of healthcare records include some form of incorrect information.[6] Meanwhile, a study from Johns Hopkins found that over 250,000 people die due to medical errors every single year in the United States. This would make it the third most common cause of death after heart disease and cancer. Those figures have been disputed, with one investigation putting them closer to 5,200. Either way, even one death is one death too many.[7]

It also is not easy to get mistakes corrected. When Gleason flagged the issue, hospital staff told her that she was the one who was mistaken. She got the record changed eventually, but it took a lot of time and effort—enough time and effort that most people would not have bothered.

One non-fatal—but still unpleasant—example of a medical error comes to us via the BBC, which reported on a woman who suffered chemical injuries after being mistakenly prescribed erectile dysfunction cream

---

[5] See: http://bit.ly/medicalrecorderrors
[6] See: http://bit.ly/medicalerrorsstats/
[7] See: http://bit.ly/johnshopkinsfactcheck

for a dry eye condition. "The woman, from Glasgow, had to be treated at A&E after she was given Vitaros cream instead of the eye lubricant VitA-POS," the BBC explains. "Her experience is detailed in December's BMJ Case Reports journal. The report calls for doctors to use block capitals in handwritten prescriptions to avoid errors."[8]

Mining Health Data

Healthcare data is vitally important, both now and in the future, and so, it is unsurprising that healthcare startups are increasingly turning their attention to the field of data mining and data capture.

One of the most interesting companies to enter the mix is China's iCarbonX, a Shenzhen-based biotechnology firm that formed an alliance with seven technology companies that specialize in capturing different types of healthcare data. The idea is to "use algorithms to analyze reams of genomic, physiological and behavioral data and provide customized health and medical advice directly to consumers through an app."[9]

iCarbonX was founded in October 2015 and has already raised more than 600 million U.S. dollars in investment, 200 million U.S. dollars of which came from WeChat owner and Chinese powerhouse Tencent. Jun Wang, the company's founder, believes that the alliance will help them to gather data more cheaply and more quickly than rivals like Google and IBM. He hopes to have samples and data from one million people within five years and to mine users' genomes "to scour biological molecules from various tissues to provide a more accurate and actionable picture of someone's health."

It is still early days for the alliance, and Wang himself has admitted that the success of the venture will depend on whether people submit their data and follow the advice that the app gives, adding, "[It] might tell me not to drink, but I don't have to listen."

Still, it is clear that there is a lot of potential to the technology, and it will be interesting to see how the burgeoning Chinese tech sector will continue to disrupt healthcare. After all, there is a real need for a solution

---

[8]   See: http://bbc.in/vitarosmixup
[9]   See: http://bit.ly/chineseaicompany

like the one that iCarbonX has to offer, and while America has historically been one of the largest global innovators when it comes to technology, China is starting to pose some serious competition—and they do not have many of the problems that hold American healthcare back.

It should not be a surprise that all of these new companies are entering the market. After all, according to a study by Grand View Research Inc., the global healthcare analytics market is set to grow from seven billion U.S. dollars in 2016 to over 53 billion U.S. dollars in 2025. In an article for Tibco, Ashwin Datla explains,

> A significant driver for this change is the shift from a fee-for-service model, where physicians are rewarded for the number of services they order, to a more value-based model, where physicians are rewarded for the value of the overall care they provide.[10]

Decentralization

The good people at Proof have made it their mission to decentralize healthcare data so that it can be accessible across all touchpoints in the healthcare system. The idea is to create an ecosystem in which data can be gathered from multiple sources and put into an overall database, which is very different to what we have at the moment.

We are gathering data all over the place. There is a huge amount of it and not just from the healthcare industry. Just look at other industries like finance if you want to see how important data can be. At the moment, it is stuck in silos, but it can and should be free. We should be learning from it.

We all know how fragmented our healthcare data is, especially over here in the United States. It is messy and it is badly managed. But, the team at Proof believes that the blockchain could be the answer. Data is valuable—it is *insanely* valuable—and it should be in the patient's hands. After all, it is their data. It belongs to them.

You can think of blockchain is being a little bit like a scalable, decentralized database that no single entity has complete ownership over. It is

---

[10] See: http://bit.ly/tibcodataanalytics

mostly known for powering cryptocurrencies, where this decentralization means that no individual bank or government has total control over the currency. The blockchain is also distributed across a number of different users, in the same way that peer-to-peer technology works, and this means that it is much more difficult for malicious users to compromise the data. In the real estate industry, a blockchain could be used to store data about properties that is realtor-agnostic and even accessible to the general public. In healthcare, it could pave the way for more interoperable healthcare records and electronic health record (EHR) systems.

At the moment, patients have no access to their data. Part of this has happened naturally just because of the way that the technology has developed, but there is also the fact that medical record providers have no incentives in place to give access to the patient. Proof's exciting new approach could be just the thing that the healthcare industry needs. I am excited to see whether it lives up to its potential.

Decentralization could help us to overcome the problem of interoperability and open up our healthcare data for the common good. The problem is that there is no overall consensus on the best way to go about it, but one potential solution is blockchain technology. PwC recently released a report in which they looked at some of the main ways that blockchain could help to modernize the healthcare industry.[11]

Supply Chain Validation

Blockchain technology could help to track supply chains and inventories and to make sure that everything is accounted for. Every single transaction will be added to the blockchain, allowing medical staff to validate their supplies with greater certainty.

Streamlining Enrolment

Enrolment, payment, and contract data take a lot of time and effort to process and to keep up-to-date. A blockchain-based system could streamline this process and allow both providers and payers to share and access

---

[11] See: http://bit.ly/pwcblockchainhealthcare

data in real time. It also makes it easier to carry out audits and can help to prevent fraud and human error. It can also save lives by speeding up reaction times and making it easier for healthcare companies to carry out treatment as quickly as possible.

Aggregating and Managing Data

This comes back to what I was saying earlier about the interoperability problems that we are coming up against. Blockchain is arguably the perfect solution, allowing data to be brought together in a centralized system and shared with people depending upon whether or not they need to access it. This would also give patients greater control over how their data is being used and allow us to take steps toward a comprehensive population health management system.

Improved Risk Tracking

Risk tracking and regulatory compliance are a big deal in the healthcare industry. The good news is that blockchain acts as an incorruptible digital ledger that keeps records on every single transaction that is made. Blockchain systems can even use smart contracts to make sure that certain actions trigger appropriate responses, including by flagging any unusual activity or by creating reports as and when they are needed.

Overpopulation

One of the biggest challenges for the future is the threat of overpopulation. The United Nations predicts that the world's population will reach 11 billion by the end of the 21st century, with 66 percent of people living in cities by 2050.[12] Over one billion people were born in the 12 years between 1999 and 2011.

On top of that, it is developing countries like India and China that represent the largest amounts of growth, but at the same time, these countries are also where there are the fewest resources available to support them. This presents both a challenge and an opportunity. After all, while

---

[12]   See: http://bit.ly/overpopulationstats

the infrastructure is not currently in place to help these countries to usher in the future of healthcare, they are also not bogged down by legacy systems that could hold them back, like much of the developed world.

Overpopulation is a hot topic at the moment, and not only because of the impact it could have on our healthcare. After all, when hospitals are overworked, understaffed, and underfunded to begin with, it is not difficult to guess what will happen as the population continues to grow. There are also huge impacts to consider when we look at the effect that we have as a species on the environment. If massive societal changes are not ushered in soon, there might not be much of a planet for us to leave behind for the ever-growing population of the future.

Luckily, there could be an answer, and that answer relies on artificial intelligence (AI) technology and the huge pools of data that we have access to. AI is being touted as a way to reduce the burden on the electricity grid[13] by spotting flaws and as a way to reduce congestion on our roads through AI-powered *robo-cars*.[14]

When it comes to healthcare, AI software could be used to great effect to manage and log resources and to avoid shortfalls as the population continues to grow and more people interact with the healthcare system. AI could also be coupled with machine learning to analyze population data and to head off healthcare issues at the pass, before they become more serious problems.

But, is that even a good thing? After all, if the population continues to grow, then providing better healthcare could exacerbate the problem by decreasing mortality rates and increasing average lifespans. You would be hard-pressed to find someone to argue that this is a bad thing, but it could also have unexpected consequences. The good news is that deploying these technologies could have other advantages, such as improving our overall quality of life, as opposed to our longevity. That is what the future of healthcare is all about.

Perhaps it is no surprise that shortly before his death, celebrated physicist Stephen Hawking warned about the dangers of AI. According to the *Daily Mirror*,[15]

---

13   See: http://bit.ly/aicleanenergy

14   See: http://bit.ly/airobocars

15   See: http://bit.ly/hawkingwarning

Mr. Hawking had recently spoken about how the "Earth was becoming too small for us" and said its exponential growth could not continue. He said if the population continued to expand in the way it has been, electricity consumption would make our planet "red hot." Mr. Hawking has also warned about the rise of powerful artificial intelligence (AI), saying it "will be either the best or the worst thing ever to happen to humanity. We do not know yet which."

The Future of Healthcare Buildings

Data will not just power the way that we treat patients. It will also change the way that the buildings we use will function and interact with the objects—and the people—inside them. It is not just the healthcare industry that has a vested interest here, which is why, it was covered on Connect Media's Commercial Real Estate blog.[16]

The article centers on a new report from Transwestern called The Future of Healthcare Buildings, which surveyed 21 different thought leaders from the healthcare industry from across the United States. It identified four main themes that we can expect from the future.

More Data

No surprises here. To quote Connect Media,

> The U.S. population already generates 2.5 quintillion bytes of data per day. Accenture estimates that the artificial intelligence (AI) health market will grow to $6.6 billion by 2021, and key clinical health AI applications could save the U.S. healthcare economy $150 billion annually by 2026.

Telemedicine

Eric Vandenbroucke, senior principal of IMEG Engineering, explains,

---

[16] See: http://bit.ly/healthcarebuildings

We will see an increase in healthcare facilities that may never see a single patient. These spaces will include facilities to support telemedicine and virtual medicine, remote monitoring of patients, and facilities that are designed to support and maintain vehicles and equipment for mobile outreach care.

Flexibility

The idea here is that we can never really know what the future will bring. That is why, contractors are starting to look at more flexible, modular healthcare buildings. "Examples of this flexibility include exam rooms, physician offices, consult rooms and procedure suites which are all built off of the same base dimensions," the report explains. "So that exam rooms may be expanded or contracted or re-purposed without any disruption to the clinic."

Decentralization

According to Connect Media,

> The move to smaller facilities will continue, along with incorporation of more services. The medical offices and clinics of the future will be smarter buildings. Patrick Casey, executive director of planning, construction and design at the University of Mississippi Medical Centre, expects that MOBs of the future will be smaller, with less lobby and waiting space. The total number of examination rooms may be reduced. The healthcare professional will need more time to work both online and virtual. And for the general practitioner, he predicts the facilities will become smaller and leaner in design, with less need for large waiting rooms, and will potentially reduce the number of exam rooms.

The Hidden Trade

Discussions and debates about how we should store and use our healthcare and medical data need to consider the fact that there are powerful vested interests who would prefer for the current system to remain in place.

Scientific American perfectly highlighted these concerns in an article called *The Hidden Trade in Our Medical Data: Why We Should Worry.*[17] "For-profit companies use our anonymized medical data in a huge secondary market," the authors explain. "Advances in computing make it increasingly possible for outsiders to identify people from among the hundreds of millions of patients in dossiers, putting intimate secrets about our bodies and minds at risk."

The vast majority of medical patients have no idea that this is even happening. Some cynics even argue that the amount of time that doctors spend filling out EHRs, coupled with their lack of interoperability and the fact that they are therefore often ineffective, essentially means that doctors are working on behalf of EHR providers instead of for the healthcare system.

It seems strange to me that we are allowing this to happen as a society when we are more focused on data and data security than ever before. *Scientific American* explains,

> Companies that have nothing to do with our medical treatment are allowed to buy and sell our healthcare data, provided they remove certain fields of information, including birth date, name and social security number. [And] a growing number of data scientists and healthcare experts say the same computing advances that allow the aggregation of millions of anonymized patient files into a dossier also make it increasingly possible to re-identify those files – that is, to match identities to patients.

To highlight the threat of re-identification, *Scientific American* quotes Jani Syed, technical group director at Management Science Associates, who said,

> In the area of big data there are always problems with privacy. No matter what you do, no matter how much data obfuscation you

---

[17] See: http://bit.ly/hiddentradeindata

are going to do, if you have enough data it is always possible to identify a particular person. It's not that hard to do.

A lot of my colleagues in the healthcare industry have an almost cavalier approach to the way that patient data is handled, simply doing the bare minimum they think they can get away with while remaining HIPAA-compliant. The thinking seems to be that they are covered as long as the data is deidentified. They also seem to think that even if people are able to tie the medical data back to personal information, there are no real applications for it, and that there is, therefore, no temptation to do it.

But, *Scientific American* disagrees, explaining,

Experts identify a variety of possible motivations for an outsider to seek to re-identify medical files. A rival at work who wants your job or simply does not like you may know when you took medical leave and other clues that could make it possible to find you in [a] batch of anonymous patient files. Suddenly, your re-identified files might appear in circulation. In a crime of passion, a romantic rival – or crossed former lover – might want to spread such information on the internet, a variant of revenge porn in which former partners post intimate photos online. Rogue investors might be keen to learn inside details about the health of key corporate leaders before stock prices react to future revelations. A fanatical sports fan may want to humiliate a rival team's star player. Medical data, both de-identified and re-identified, could also become national security weapons against members of the armed forces and their families, or high-ranking officers.

Data for Pharmaceuticals

In the future, there is every chance that pharmaceutical companies will use a combination of AI and big data to simulate the impact that new drugs could have before they are released into the wild. It is true that a certain amount of testing has to take place before a new drug is approved by the Food and Drug Administration (FDA) and its global equivalents, but even the most thorough clinical trials pale into insignificance when compared against complex modeling covering millions of different data points.

In an article for McKinsey, Thibaut Dedeurwaerder, Daniele Iacovelli, Eoin Leydon, and Parag Patel explain, "The technology exists today – including predictive analytics, robotic process automation, and AI-based tools, all digitally connected via the Internet of Things (IoT) – but no pharma company has fully leveraged it."[18]

It is the same old problem that we are used to from other industries. Adopting new technologies is not easy, and many companies end up using individual tools without a cohesive approach that brings them all together. Part of the problem is that new tech initiatives get stuck in the pilot phase or take too long to show results, especially for money-oriented CEOs who are quick to pull the plug when it does not look like something is working. But, just like with marketing, it takes time for these things to deliver a return, and risk-averse pharmaceutical companies often lack the visionaries that are needed to make the potential of these systems a reality.

One of the biggest opportunities for pharmaceutical companies is the potential for real-time predictive analytics. The idea is to use both historic and current data to predict what is likely to happen in any given set of circumstances. This allows drug companies to spot problems before they occur and to take steps to avoid them in what is effectively the corporate equivalent of preventative healthcare. Why wait until something goes wrong if you can head it off at the pass?

According to the McKinsey article,

Companies can also build digital simulations of production processes – on the level of individual machines, labs, factories, or entire manufacturing networks. These real-time digital "twin" simulations allow companies to steer processes proactively by predicting the effect of adding a new machine, changing schedules, or changing the team allocation – all before applying those steps to physical assets. In this way, the company can optimize pro-

---

[18] See: https://mck.co/2PLGaqx

duction parameters for highly complex systems, accurately and proactively, without risk. This is a significant advance in efficiency compared to the traditional approach of sifting through historical data manually to try to spot trends.

The biggest weakness in pharmaceutical production is the risk of human error, in part because tasks performed by humans are typically only 92 percent accurate. That is why, major industries are increasingly relying on automation and AI, and it is also why self-driving cars are statistically much safer than manually driven cars. Software does not get tired, lose focus, or show up to work with a hangover.

"The shop floor is increasingly digital," Dedeurwaerder explains,

powered by new systems that support operators in daily tasks, particularly those that are highly repetitive. For example, tools such as augmented-reality glasses could show operators the checklist of steps needed to finish specific processes, or confirm that required measures have been completed, along with gathering and reporting data to fuel analytical models. Managers could also be given a tablet-based dashboard with real-time performance KPIs, losses, machine status, and potential measures to improve. If something goes wrong – or is likely to go wrong – the managers receive an alert.

Black Box Health

I have a vision of the future that I would like to share with you. You have probably heard of black boxes before because they are used in planes and other vehicles to monitor everything that happens. When a plane crashes, investigators look for the black box so that they can identify what happened. Similar technologies power telematics devices, which can be installed in cars and used to gain insights into how they are being driven. Some car insurers now base their customers' premiums on the data that they receive from the telematics device.

Let us take a look at the recent Lion Air crash as an example. Flight JT610 was a Boeing 737 that crashed toward the end of October 2018, killing all 1,899 people on board. The black box was recovered four days after the plane disappeared from radar, and then divers switched their focus to finding the cockpit voice recorder. The black box is so important that Captain Daniel Putut Kuncoro Adi, the managing director of Lion Group, refused to offer any possible explanations for the crash until the black box data had been accessed and analyzed, a process that takes three or more months to complete.[19]

Imagine for a moment what would happen if every single human being had a black box of their own. The data that it generated would feed into our healthcare record systems and lead to more comprehensive data on every single one of us as individuals, as well as the health of the global population as a whole. Then, if a patient got sick, had an adverse reaction, or died because of an illness or a course of treatment, we would be able to look at their personal black box and identify what caused it.

Much of my focus in the field of medicine is around the concept of personalized medicine, in which every single one of us receives tailored suggestions throughout our life based upon data gathered from wearable devices, our medical histories, and tailored suggestions based on the treatment plans and the outcomes of other, similar patients.

This idea of each of us having a *black box* that stores all of our data could be brought about by new technologies like blockchain, which have the ability to power decentralized systems that give the data back to the patients themselves and not to whichever EHR company happens to own the data. For the future of healthcare to become a reality, we need access to more data, and we need it to be fully interoperable. A blockchain-based black box system could be the solution that we have all been looking for.

Are We Ready?

We have reached a pivotal point in time at which we already have the possibility to create an *Internet of People* through everything from smartwatches and other wearables to electronic implants. But, this comes with an interesting quandary when it comes to who will have ownership and access to the data that we create. In an article for the *Wall Street Journal*,

19   See: http://cnn.it/lionaircrashblackbox

professor of law and computer science Dr. Andrea Matwyshyn argues, "Using the human body as a technology platform raises a host of challenging legal and policy questions that regulators and judges may not be prepared to answer."[20]

On top of the technologies and devices that we already know about and have access to, we can expect much more to come from the future. Examples include smart tattoos that monitor patients' vital signs or Internet-connected contact lenses. This is all well and good and bodes well for the future of healthcare, but there are all sorts of legal and ethical questions that are also raised when dealing with the kind of sensitive data that the healthcare industry relies upon.

"For the first time," Dr. Matwyshyn explains, "our physical safety, autonomy, and well-being can – and inevitably will – be harmed because of flawed software or lapses in security. Yet the law is unprepared to address the injuries that the Internet of Bodies will bring."

This reminds me of a similar debate in the field of AI: namely, the debate behind who is responsible if a patient dies as a result of a flawed recommendation by a piece of software. As for the Internet of People, Matwyshyn highlights five key areas of concern that we, as a society, need to address:

Regulatory Issues

The FDA does not necessarily cover wearable devices like fitness trackers. In many cases, oversight would fall to the Federal Trade Commission, a much smaller agency that has neither the resources nor the expertise that is needed.

Intellectual Property

One of the big threats here is that of the patent troll, which is essentially when someone buys up patents to make money by enforcing them as opposed to using them to develop a product or service. Another issue is that companies could develop proprietary systems and then go out of

---

[20] See: http://on.wsj.com/internetofbodies

business, leaving patients implanted with medical devices that are no longer supported.

Contract Law

We are so used to accepting license agreements and privacy policies these days that we rarely stop to read the small print. The problem is that if we follow a similar model when using devices for our bodies, we could sign away more than we intend to. An example of this is when companies brick a device unless the user accepts the latest changes to the licensing agreement. Will they be able to do the same even if we have been implanted with a physical device?

Bankruptcy

Historically, contract rights and databases have been treated as assets during bankruptcy. But, what will happen if a prosthetics manufacturer goes bust? And, who will have access to that data? These are questions that we need to ask ourselves now instead of waiting until it is too late.

It may seem as though I am getting ahead of myself here. After all, some would say that it is too early to start worrying about the ethical implications of new technologies when the technologies themselves are yet to reach fruition. The problem is that it is never a good idea to leave things to the last minute, especially when it comes to something as important as our healthcare, and so, we should have these conversations now so that we can prepare ourselves.

Besides, perhaps the future is not as far away as you first thought. Take the case of John Hancock, one of the oldest, biggest life insurers in North America. According to NBC News, the company "will stop underwriting traditional life insurance and instead sell only interactive policies that track fitness and health data through wearable devices and smartphones."[21] They are also allowing existing customers to opt-in, and it is an interesting move by the company. Requiring customers to provide access to their data in exchange for a service is usually a bad idea, but at

---

[21] See: http://nbcnews.to/johnhancockwearables

the same time, it will allow the company to provide much more accurate insurance plans. It might even save people some money.

Matwyshyn's point about our readiness to embrace the future is echoed by an article by Andrew Jack in *The Financial Times*, where he talks about impact investing in digital health. "Others raise different concerns around digital innovation," Jack explains.

> One is about privacy and safety, notably where individuals' identities and medical conditions are linked to their location, for example, in zones of political insecurity. Another is interoperability, as a surge in electronic health systems being developed by different companies leads to a proliferation of data that might rely heavily on a supplier and be incompatible with other systems. Also of concern is the danger of poor quality of measurement and collection of data, which limits the capacity to generate meaningful information, without which efforts at machine learning and artificial intelligence will be hampered. There is little doubt that technology businesses can help improve the health of the poorest. But investors need to be sensitive to their limitations and alternative or complementary ways to generate impact.[22]

The Downsides of Data

Creating data costs money, while storing it and processing it require huge amounts of resources, which also do not come cheap. On top of that, healthcare data is more sensitive than most, making security paramount and regulatory compliance a necessity. And, because of the sheer size of the medical industry and the number of different companies that work within it, the number of vulnerabilities and potential entry points are quite simply off the charts.

One example of this was covered in *Business Insider*, which explained,

---

[22] See: http://on.ft.com/impactinvestingarticle

As millions of Americans sat down to Thanksgiving dinner, bio-medical researcher James Hazel sent out a stark warning about the genetic testing kits that he surmised would be a hot topic of conversation. Most of them are neither safe nor private.[23]

Hazel had reviewed privacy policies and terms of service pages for nearly 100 different genetic testing companies, "from popular start-ups like 23andMe – which offers health and ancestry information – to under-the-radar outfits such as GEDmatch, which simply houses genetic information to help people to build family trees." Ultimately, he discovered that nearly half of them did not even have a basic privacy document.

The article also shares some statistics, explaining that Ancestry has sold 14 million DNA kits, while 23andMe stores genetic data on more than five million customers. But, perhaps more shocking is the case of the Golden State Killer, a man called Joseph DeAngelo who was arrested on multiple charges, thanks to DNA. *Business Insider* says,

At some point, 24 people distantly related to him uploaded their genetic data to a public DNA database called GEDmatch. After creating a fake GEDmatch profile using DNA they'd gathered at the scene of a 1980 crime, investigators were led to those people. By cross-checking the list against several other databases such as census data and cemetery records, they were able to close in on DeAngelo.

This phenomenon is known as *reidentification*, and it is a real threat wherever large amounts of anonymized data is stored in a single place. On top of that, it opens up all sorts of ethical questions. In this case, the arrest of a serial killer might not seem like such a bad thing, but the same thing could happen in other instances. We are yet to see the full implications of these technologies, but they do pose a serious threat to our anonymity if nothing else.

---

[23] See: http://bit.ly/dnafuturebusinessinsider

Data Breaches

Because healthcare is such a high-profile industry with access to huge amounts of valuable data, it is also one of the most prone to attacks, hacks, and data breaches. This is highlighted in a recent study which found that "healthcare entities have reported the highest number of data breaches of any industry for figures relating to 2018."[24]

The report, The Beazley Breach Insights Report, concluded that 41 percent of healthcare bodies had been affected by data breaches, and that the causes ranged from direct hacking and the presence of malware to human error (such as poor passwords or people falling victim to phishing scams).

Still, it is not all bad news. Reporting on the findings, Digital Journal explained, "The general trend with healthcare, as with other sectors, was for hacking and malware incidents to be increasing and for unintended disclosures to be decreasing, which may signal improvements to internal practices and with business culture."

So ultimately, it is something of a double-edged sword. Healthcare companies are getting better at providing their employees with the training they need to keep their data safe, but attackers are getting more sophisticated. It is essentially a digital arms race, and it is consumers' healthcare data that is at stake.

That means that for us, as medical professionals, we have a duty of care to go out of our way to ensure that patient data is stored as securely as possible. This will only become more important as we continue to store more and more data. It is also going to cost a lot of money and consume huge amounts of resources, but it will be worth it. And ultimately, for the future of healthcare to come about, it will just have to happen.

Digital Exceptionalism

Has AI's capacity to process all of this data been over exaggerated? I am a big believer in the power of AI to revolutionize our society, and our healthcare system is no different. That said, it is far from perfect. For example, researchers in Korea analyzed literature evaluating 516 AI algorithms for

---

[24]   See: http://bit.ly/healthcaredatabreaches

medical image analysis and found that only 6 percent validated their AI and 0 percent were ready for clinical use. Lack of appropriate clinical validation is called digital exceptionalism.

Seong Ho Park, MD, PhD of Seoul's University of Ulsan College of Medicine explained,

> Nearly all of the studies published in the study period that eval-
> uated the performance of AI algorithms for diagnostic analysis
> of medical images were designed as proof-of-concept technical
> feasibility studies and didn't have the design features that are rec-
> ommended for robust validation of the real-world clinical perfor-
> mance of AI algorithms.

In the studies' defense, not all of them were designed to test the real-world readiness of AI. In fact, some of them were designed to rule out options or to test the feasibility of a given method. That said, the research-ers noted that in the future, radiologists and researchers should take it upon themselves to understand the differences between proof-of-concept studies and those meant to validate the clinical performance of AI in the real world.

For algorithms to be tested for image analysis, a study must include diagnostic cohort design, inclusion of multiple institutions, and prospec-tive data collection for external validation. Ideally, studies would also have access to large amounts of data so that they can ensure that any results are not just statistical anomalies.

Ultimately, though, the Korean researchers were pessimistic, concluding,

> Our results reveal that most recently published studies reporting
> the performance of AI algorithms for diagnostic analysis of med-
> ical images did not have design features that are recommended
> for robust validation of the clinical performance of AI algorithms,
> confirming the worries that premier journals have recently raised.[25]

---

[25] See: http://bit.ly/digitalexceptionalism

Leaks

Hacks, leaks, and breaches are almost daily occurrences, and so many of them happened while I was writing this book that it was impossible for me to keep track of all of them. One of the most notable was a high-profile breach at Facebook, which exposed the e-mails of nearly one billion people, in what is believed to be the biggest data breach of all time.[26]

But, as bad as e-mail leaks can be, they pale into insignificance compared to what could happen if it was our medical data that was compromised. It sounds like a nightmare situation, but it is something that is already happening and which could become more and more common in the months and years to come. Just one example of a healthcare data breach was covered by TechCrunch's Zack Whittaker, who explained, "A health tech company was leaking thousands of doctor's notes, medical records and prescriptions after a security lapse left a server without a password."[27]

The issue was brought to light by SpiderSilk, a Dubai-based cybersecurity firm, and affected a relatively obscure electronic medical record company called Meditab. Whittaker explains,

> The company, among other things, processes electronic faxes for healthcare providers, still a primary method for sharing patient files to other providers and pharmacies. But that fax server wasn't properly secured. Because the server had no password, anyone could read the transmitted faxes in real-time – including their contents. The faxes contained a host of personally identifiable information and health information, including medical records, doctor's notes, prescription amounts and quantities, as well as illness information, such as blood test results. The faxes also included names, addresses, dates of birth and in some cases Social Security numbers, health insurance information and payment data.

---

[26]   See: http://bit.ly/facebookleaksonebillion
[27]   See: http://bit.ly/medicalrecordsexposed

Stories like these should act as timely reminders of the importance of cybersecurity in the healthcare industry, but the sad truth is that they will never be unavoidable. It is a cat-and-mouse game, with researchers and cybersecurity professionals constantly trying to outwit the malicious actors who breach systems and hold data to ransom. But, while we might not be able to stop these leaks from ever happening, we can at least take steps to reduce their likelihood and then hold companies responsible for communicating any breaches as quickly and openly as possible.

Wellness Culture

More data is a good thing, right? After all, the idea is that we will be healthier if we have more information about our habits, bodily functions, and biological predispositions. But in an interesting thought piece for NBC News, Canada Research Chair in Health Law and Policy at the University of Alberta Timothy Caulfield argues otherwise.

"A lot of the new data suggests our technology isn't transforming us into a generation of street-dancing, step-maximising, sleep-mastering tri-athletes," Caulfield says.

> No surprise. Behavior change is hard. And the quantification craze may also be making life a little less enjoyable. A series of studies published in 2016 found that measuring activities can make them feel more like work, and, consequently, less fun. As a result, the push to quantify life, the study author concluded, has the potential to decrease the continued engagement in an activity and, worse, adversely impact our overall wellbeing.[28]

The crux of Caulfield's argument is that tracking data will only get you so far, and if we do not actually act on that data, then it is essentially ineffective. Perhaps, Caulfield is just a pessimist, but it could also be that he is a realist. He explains,

---

[28]   See: http://bit.ly/wellnessculture

Study after study after study has found that providing genetic predisposition information to individuals – even when paired with professional counselling – does not produce meaningful or sustained behavior change. The science regarding the health benefits of fitness trackers is also remarkably underwhelming. Some studies have found a short-term positive bump in exercise when people start using activity trackers. Long term, however, the benefits often dissipate. But more concerning is the evidence that suggest that for some groups, using a fitness tracker might result in worse health outcomes. For example, a relatively large and long-term clinical trial found that research participants wearing fitness trackers lost significantly less weight than the research participants who weren't. Another study found that for adolescents, fitness trackers were demoralizing, largely because the devices added a peer-pressure, competitive vibe to physical activity.

Caulfield summarizes his thoughts by saying he votes for less data, more living, and cautioning us against being *fooled* by the *flashy marketing* and the *intuitive appeal of the quantification trend*. He says, "We don't need personalized genetic information or an activity monitor to remind us of the benefits of exercise, eating real food and getting a good night's sleep. And if you want to dance in the street, dance in the street."

Building on from Caulfield, I would like to bring your attention to a piece by Stacey Higginbotham in which she talked about how many wearables and healthcare apps are nothing more than digital snake oil. And, while it may seem like an extreme position to hold for someone who is involved in the digital health space, I think she has a point.

Higginbotham says we should draw a line between digital wellness and digital medicine, explaining,

Today, consumers and doctors are bombarded with claims. Apple says the Apple Watch can detect if the person wearing it is going into atrial fibrillation. Researchers believe they have developed an app that can tell if you're depressed simply by monitoring how you type and interact with the screen. Companies are pushing home versions of medical devices for detecting respiratory diseases in children, spotting chronic obstructive pulmonary disease, and testing urine that all claim to deliver clinical data. In the United States, the Food and Drug Administration has clamped down on a few offending apps, such as several that purport to diagnose concussions. But there are plenty of devices that straddle the line between digital wellness and actual digital medicine.[29]

What the Data Says

I recently came across a report by Stanford University (their 2017 Health Trends Report)[30] that aimed to highlight some of the themes that are shaping the future of healthcare. "With the cost of care on the rise," the authors explained, "the industry is experiencing a shift towards preventative and value-based care. At the same time, technology like wearable devices, at-home testing services and telemedicine are empowering patients to be more engaged with and proactive about their own health."

Speaking of telemedicine, I was pleased to see a recent piece by *The Times* that outlined former U.K. Prime Minister Theresa May's plans to make Skype consultations with hospital doctors the new norm in the National Health Service. According to *The Times*, the plan will impact millions of patients and reduce face-to-face consultations by a third, saving the cash-strapped NHS billions of pounds in the process. "30 million hospital visits a year will be avoided by use of Skype calls, smartphones and other ways to talk to a doctor," the article concludes.[31]

But, let us get back to that Stanford University report. "Beyond these trends is one fundamental force driving healthcare transformation," it explains. "The power of data." Data is used across every aspect of the

[29] See: http://bit.ly/digitalsnakeoilwearables
[30] See: http://stan.md/healthtrendsreport
[31] See: http://bit.ly/nhsskypeplan

healthcare industry, from medical research to monitoring diagnostics during patients' day-to-day lives. Machine learning is already as good as or better than many human physicians at diagnosing illnesses. The data can also be used to "build better patient profiles and predictive models to more effectively anticipate, diagnose and treat disease."

Stanford also highlighted several of the main challenges that healthcare companies will have to face, ranging from spiraling costs to the security of data and the lack of legislative framework. Then, there is the growing dissatisfaction that physicians have for electronic medical records (EMRs) and the lack of skills and training, especially among more traditionally conservative areas of the healthcare industry.

When it comes to preventative healthcare, the authors of the report noted,

> Reliance on reactive healthcare will hamper physicians' ability to anticipate, diagnose and treat disease. [In the future], patients will no longer need to feel physical illness to prompt them to seek medical attention. The promise of wearables is in the ability to detect and therefore treat illness at an earlier stage. Soon, medical centers, rather than tech and fitness companies, will become the de facto providers of wearables. In fact, a majority of people already agree that they would be excited to experience wearable technology from a doctor (65%), from a hospital (62%) or a health insurance company (62%).

The Stanford University report is also interesting because of a couple of standout statistics. The first is a chart showing the annual average number of doctor visits per person across seven different countries. Japan takes the top spot with 13, followed by Germany (9.7), Canada (7.4), France (6.8), and Australia (6.7). At the bottom, the United States (4.1) and the United Kingdom (5).

I also appreciated that the report highlighted another study from the *Journal of General Internal Medicine* that showed "a cost reduction of over $3,600 for patients that experienced [a] care transition intervention." This study shows that inpatient readmission costs can be markedly reduced through a preventative approach toward healthcare.

Susan Potter Will Live Forever

"Susan Potter donated her body to science," National Geographic says.

It was frozen, sawed into four blocks, sliced 27,000 times, and photographed after each cut. The result: a virtual cadaver that will speak to medical students from the grave. For the last 15 years of her life, Potter carried a card with these words: "It is my wish to have my body used for purposes similar to those used in the Visible Human Project, namely that photographic images might be used on the Internet for medical education. In the event of my death, page Dr. Victor M. Spitzer, Ph.D. There is a four-hour window for the remains to be received."[32]

Susan knew before she died what would happen to her body. She had visited where the body would be taken, examined the machinery, and spent time talking to Dr. Spitzer to understand exactly what he wanted to do. Spitzer and his assistant eventually used a crosscut saw to cut Potter's body into four sections as the first step toward turning her body into a digital avatar that can talk *to m*edical students and help them to understand how the human body is put together.

"Dissection of a cadaver is like an archaeological excavation," the article says. "To get to the deepest layers, one works from the top down. The process is anxiety provoking and enthralling – a medical school initiation rite with almost religious overtones."

The problem is that with the rise of new technologies, more and more time is being spent focusing on other areas. "In the early 20th century," the article says,

medical students spent a thousand hours studying anatomy. Now it's no more than 150 hours. A cadaver is a costly, nonrenewable resource. Medical schools don't pay for cadavers but do pay for transportation, embalming and storage. The 24 bodies used in the

---

[32] See: http://on.natgeo.com/susanpotter

anatomy lab at the University of Colorado School of Medicine cost $1,900 each.

The idea behind Spitzer's project was to create a virtual cadaver that could be repeatedly dissected and then restored to life. To do this, they had to slice bodies up until they were millimeter thin and then to photograph each section so that they could all be combined and turned into a precise digital copy of the human anatomy.

Imagine if we donated our data in a similar manner. Imagine if we could bring it together from different providers and share it with researchers so that they could study how it signals health issues ahead of time.

When I shared this article from my LinkedIn profile, my friend Grace Cordovano, PhD, BCPA, posted a comment to say,

> Fascinating, mind-boggling, gut-wrenching. Exceptional story and reporting. Thanks for sharing. I've openly discussed data donation after death, as a part of advanced directives and advanced care planning. Patients need access and control to make those decisions. Aside from donating for advancement of human data science, what a powerful gift to pass on to one's children and family. Talk about the ultimate family tree!

This is exactly my vision of the future of healthcare. The gift of data will enable us to take personalized healthcare to another level.

Giving Patients Control of Their Health

Dr. Ran Balicer, the director of the Clalit Research Institute in Israel, recently gave a talk at Singularity University's Exponential Medicine conference in San Diego. Writing about the event for the University's SingularityHub, neuroscientist Shelly Fan said,

> [Dr. Balicer] painted a futuristic picture of how big data can merge with personalized healthcare into an app-based system in which the patient is in control. Picture this: instead of going to a physician with your ailments, your doctor calls you with some

bad news: "Within six hours, you're going to have a heart attack. So why don't you come into the clinic and we can fix that?' Crisis averted."[33]

The general idea is that patients should be given the tools and knowledge that they need to monitor their biomarkers, lab test results, and other information. Through the smart use of mobile applications, patients would be able to track their health over the long term. They could even set health goals within the app.

"With this hefty dose of AI," Fan explains,

You're in charge of your health – in fact, probably more so than under current healthcare systems. Sound fantastical? In fact, [Dr. Balicer says that] this type of preemptive care is already being provided in some countries, including Israel, at a massive scale. By mining datasets with deep learning and other powerful AI tools, we can predict the future – and put it into the hands of patient.

One of the reasons why Israel is leading the way here is the fact that it already has access to a huge database containing "decades of electronic health records aggregated within a central warehouse [and] a wealth of health-related data on the scale of millions of people and billions of data points." According to Fan, "The data is incredibly multiplex, covering lab tests, drugs, hospital admissions, medical procedures and more."

This is an advantage that the United States cannot compete with, thanks to the fragmentation of our EHRs. This is also why I like to think that the future will be decentralized, which would give more power to patients by releasing the data that is currently held hostage. Over in Israel, Dr. Balicer has been able to develop algorithms to predict diabetes, winter pneumonia, osteoporosis, and more.

And of course, when you are able to predict these problems, you can take steps to treat the illness before it becomes a major problem. This is echoed by Shelly Fan, who says, "A particularly powerful use of AI in

---

[33] See: http://bit.ly/controlyourhealth

medicine is to bring insights and trends directly to the patient, such that they can take control over their own health and medical care."

Another example of AI's potential comes to us via the problem of drug dosing. Our present healthcare system uses doses that are based on the average results across all patients during clinical trials. By contrast, an AI-based system could make dosage recommendations based on the best dosages for other, similar patients. Fan explains, "Such personalized recommendations are beyond the ability of any single human doctor. But with the help of AI, which can quickly process massive datasets to find similarities, doctors may soon be able to prescribe individually-tailored medications."

"We built thousands of models for each patient to comprehensively understand the impact of the treatment for the individual," Dr. Balicer adds.

> For example, a reduced risk for stroke and cardiovascular-related deaths could be accompanied by an increase in serious renal failure. This approach [leads to] a truly personalized balance, allowing patients and their physicians to ultimately decide if the risks of the treatment are worth the benefits. We are not the sum of our biologics and medical stats. A truly personalized approach needs to take a patient's needs and goals and the sacrifices and tradeoffs they're willing to make into account, rather than having the physician make decisions for them. Health systems will not be replaced by algorithms, rest assured, but health systems that don't use algorithms will be replaced by those that do.

Welcome to the future of healthcare.

CHAPTER 7

Artificial Intelligence in Healthcare

Some people call this artificial intelligence, but the reality is this technology will enhance us. So instead of artificial intelligence, I think we'll augment our intelligence.

—*Ginni Rometty*

I have built a career out of talking about how artificial intelligence (AI), machine learning, and other technologies can revolutionize the field of healthcare. What I do not always talk about is how they could revolutionize the field of competitive gaming. Google's DeepMind has taught itself to play a number of Atari games, including Atari Breakout, and YouTuber SethBling has created a cleverly named program called *MarI/O*, which uses "neural networks and genetic algorithms [to kick] butt at Super Mario World."

Another use of AI comes to us via Google's AI team, which has recently discovered "a new method for teaching computers to understand why some images are more aesthetically pleasing than others." It is called neural image assessment (NIMA), and it relies on deep learning to train a convolutional neural network (CNN) to predict ratings for different images. And, as TheNextWeb explains,

The NIMA model eschews traditional approaches in favor of a 10-point rating scale. A machine examines both the specific pixels of an image and its overall aesthetic. It then determines how likely any rating is to be chosen by a human.

It might not seem like this has much to do with healthcare, but it is important to remember that AI is still a new field, and advances in one industry can often be applied to another. In this case, a variant of the NIMA model could be used to determine which patients need the most immediate treatment.

According to a paper from the NIMA project's researchers,

> [Our] approach differs from others in that we predict the distribution of human opinion scores using a convolutional neural network. Our resulting network can be used to not only score images reliably and with high correlation to human perception, but also to assist with adaptation and optimization of photo editing/enhancement algorithms in a photographic pipeline.

In other words, it could help photographers to sort through photos and determine which ones are the best.

Let us face it—AI is cool. But, it is more than just some flashy new technology; indeed, it is decades old, although it is only recently that we have been able to harness it for the good of global healthcare. I truly believe that AI will universalize healthcare and remove borders between countries. It will usher in a future that we could hardly have dreamed about back in 1971, when Médecins Sans Frontières was first established. Health data from people in third-world countries and developed countries could all be part of one huge database with AI algorithms to personalize care and offer an equal standard of healthcare all over the globe. The Internet has already opened up the borders, and when you open up the data—or any data, for that matter—to unsupervised machine learning, the potential for positive change is greater than ever.

Lowering the Cost of Prediction

I recently came across a fascinating talk by University of Toronto professor Ajay Agrawal, where he hit upon one of AI's underrated (but highly important) benefits: it helps to lower the cost of prediction.

Economics is beyond the scope of this book, and indeed, there are no shortage of tomes out there that cover the economic impact of AI and the so-called *prediction machines*. Writing about Agrawal's talk, McKinsey Publishing's senior managing editor Rik Kirkland explains,

We can look at the example of another technology, semiconductors, to understand the profound changes that occur when technology drops the cost of a useful input. Semiconductors reduced the cost of arithmetic, and as they did this, three things happened. First, we started using more arithmetic for applications that already leveraged arithmetic as an input. Second, we started using this cheaper arithmetic to solve problems that hadn't traditionally been framed as arithmetic problems. The third thing that happened as the cost of arithmetic fell was that it changed the value of other things—the value of arithmetic's complements went up and the value of its substitutes went down. So, in the case of photography, the complements were the software and hardware used in digital cameras. The value of these increased because we used more of them, while the value of substitutes, the components of film-based cameras, went down because we started using less and less of them.[1]

Viewing—not to mention AI—in this way can be a game-changer, and yet, it is often missed in discussions in AI in healthcare because by definition, few healthcare specialists are also qualified economists. When it comes to AI algorithms, which Agrawal calls *prediction machines*, a drop in the cost of predictions will make it more appealing for AI to be used for more traditional prediction problems, which in the healthcare industry could include the likelihood of illnesses within the patient population, because predictions will become faster, cheaper, and more accurate.

Prediction problems could well be more widespread than you might initially think. "For example," Kirkland says,

we never thought of autonomous driving as a prediction problem. Traditionally, engineers programmed an autonomous vehicle to move around in a controlled environment, such as a factory or warehouse, by telling it what to do in certain situations—if a human walks in front of the vehicle (then stop) or if a shelf is

---

[1] See: http://bit.ly/aieconomics

empty (then move to the next shelf). But we could never put those vehicles on a city street because there are too many ifs—if it's dark, if it's rainy, if a child runs into the street, if an oncoming vehicle has its blinker on. No matter how many lines of code we write, we couldn't cover all the potential ifs.

But, if we reframe autonomous cars as a prediction problem, instead of relying on a brute force approach, an AI can predict the answer to what a qualified human driver might do. Kirkland says,

> To teach an AI drive, we put a human in a vehicle and tell the human to drive while the AI is figuratively sitting beside the human, watching. Since the AI doesn't have eyes and ears like we do, we give it cameras, radar, and light detection and ranging (LIDAR). The AI takes the input data as it comes in through its "eyes" and looks over to the human and tries to predict, "What will the human do next?"

This is one of the simplest, but most accurate descriptions of AI that I have ever come across, and we are not ever yet. Kirkland continues,

> The AI makes a lot of mistakes at first. But it learns from its mistakes and updates its model every time it incorrectly predicts an action the human will take. Its predictions start getting better and better until it becomes so good at predicting what a human would do that we don't need the human to do it anymore. The AI can perform the action itself.

As for the economic effect of all this, Agrawal and Kirkland's conclusion is surprisingly simple: "The main substitute for machine prediction is human prediction." As machine prediction gets cheaper and more accessible—not to mention much better than we can expect from humans, who are error-prone and more vulnerable to bias—AI will take on those prediction-based roles that humans are no longer suited for. And, while it does this, the data that it uses to operate will become more and more valuable, while debates erupt about who actually owns our data and how we can best protect it. I will be writing about this at length in an upcoming book called *Who Owns Our Data?*

Of course, humans have other abilities, such as their creativity and their ability to exercise judgment. An example of this is when AI is used to predict demand for perishable foods, which will not do much good without retailers who pay attention and make purchasing decisions accordingly.

"We've never really unbundled those aspects of decision making before," Kirkland says.

> We usually think of human decision making as a single step. Now we're unbundling decision making. The machine's doing the prediction, making the distinct role of judgment in decision making clearer. So as the value of human prediction falls, the value of human judgment goes up because AI doesn't do judgment—it can only make predictions and then hand them off to a human to use his or her judgment to determine what to do with those predictions.

Agrawal and Kirkland end the article with a list of things that business leaders can do to better position their companies to take advantage of AI and prediction machines:

1. Develop a thesis on time to AI impact
2. Recognize that AI progress will likely be exponential
3. Trust the machines
4. Know what you want to predict
5. Manage the learning loop

Hebb's Rule

One of the most rapidly growing areas of AI is that of artificial neural networks (ANNs), a subcategory of AI software that aims to provide a "very rough model of how the human brain is structured." ANNs have a long and rich history which dates back to the 1960s, but they have only recently become a feasible technology, thanks to an increase in computer processing power and the amount of data that we have available to train them.

ANNs do not use "explicit knowledge stored as rules of operation." Instead, they use "implicit knowledge that's encoded in numeric parameters – called weights – and distributed over many connections." They follow a piece of logic known as Hebb's rule, which states that every time a correct decision is made, the neural pathways must be reinforced.

This works through a process called supervised learning. According to an article by staffers from Josh.ai on Medium,

> We essentially ask them a large number of questions and provide them with answers. With enough examples of question-answer pairs, the calculations and values stored at each neuron and synapse are slowly adjusted. Usually this is through a process called backpropagation.

AI is one of those interesting fields in which it is easy to grasp the basic concepts, but where the underlying data science is difficult for a human being to comprehend. Luckily, the Medium article has a great example:

> Imagine you're walking down a sidewalk and you see a lamp post. You've never seen a lamp post before, so you walk right into it and say "ouch." The next time you see a lamp post, you scoot a few inches to the side and keep walking. This time, your shoulder hits the lamp post and again you say "ouch." The third time you see a lamp post, you move all the way over to ensure you don't hit the lamp post. Except now something terrible has happened – now you've walked directly into the path of a mailbox, and you've never seen a mailbox before. You walk into it and the whole process happens again. Obviously, this is an oversimplification, but it's effectively what backpropagation does.

ANNs have developed still further. The new trend is for recurrent neural networks (RNNs) that address an inherent design flaw in typical ANNs. The article explains that "a typical ANN [learns] to make decisions based on context in training, but once it was making decisions for use, the decisions were made independent of each other." This fails to address naturally changing variables. So, for example, if an ANN was used to play poker, it would forget which cards had already been played between every hand. An RNN would know exactly which cards remain in the deck and adjust its decisions accordingly.

AI for EHRs

One of the most exciting new uses of AI—when it comes to healthcare, at least—is the potential for it to revolutionize our struggling electronic health record (her) system. And, it is easy to see why.

I have talked before about how insane it is that doctors spend over two-thirds of their time filling out paperwork when they could be spending that time with their patients. One recent report by Medscape, which is owned by WebMD, found that doctors spend an average of 13–16 minutes per patient. Meanwhile, many people are worried that their conditions are not serious enough to warrant professional help, so they keep their complaints to themselves, instead of risking wasting their physician's time. Patients are well aware of the shortage of time that doctors face. Those who were interviewed for the study talked about "the pressured context in which their consultations take place: the limited resources, the lack of time, and busy doctors."

The balance is actually getting worse over time. About 10 years ago, doctors *only* spent an average of one-third of their time on the paperwork. The problem is now so big that it is having a serious impact on the level of treatment that patients can expect. As TheNextWeb reports,

In 2014, a health IT solutions designer named Jess Jacobs started keeping track of all the hours she spent at her hospital. She found that only 29% of her 56 outpatient doctor visits were useful. On average, she had to wait 20 hours to get a bed in the hospital. Other calculations showed that just 0.08% of her time being hospitalized was spent treating her conditions. Jacobs, who suffered from two rare diseases, passed away in 2016, which made her message all the more poignant.

Milan Petkovic, head of the data science department at Philips Research, believes that increasing productivity and saving time is one of the biggest advantages that medical AI solutions have to offer, explaining, "Doctors will provide better diagnoses and treatments with less time and effort, making healthcare much more efficient."

The future of AI in healthcare is bright indeed, but there is a long way to go before we get there. We need to solve the problems with today's EHRs before we can even think about the sweeping improvements that AI could usher in.

Problematic EHR systems are exacerbated by prior authorization, which is effectively a rationing tool that insurance companies use. It does this by forcing patients and physicians to fill out a bunch of forms. These are submitted to the insurance company to decide whether to reimburse the patient for the physician's recommended treatment option.

When it comes to EHRs, physicians and medical facilities essentially have no choice and are forced to spend huge amounts of time entering data. That patient data can then be sold at a profit to the EHR company—but physicians and patients do not see the benefit.

That is where AI could come in. After all, EHRs are not an inherently bad idea, and humanity as a whole could reap huge rewards from the data if only it was easy to gather and to share. The use of AI for EHRs would solve both of these issues by standardizing healthcare records and by gathering data on the doctor's behalf.

These AI EHR systems could even integrate directly with insurance companies' prior authorization systems, making it quicker and easier for physicians to decide upon the best course of action while still sticking to the budget that is available to the patient via their insurer.

It might not be perfect, especially in the early days when the AI is still using machine learning to make sense of the data that is available to it, but it is a start. And, it is certainly better than the cumbersome system that we use at the moment in which we are wasting time and resources to create records that do not add any value.

Speaking of EHRs, Epic CEO Judy Faulkner, who recently argued with Joe Biden about whether patients should have access to their own records, believes that we are soon to see a switch from EHRs to comprehensive health records (CHRs). She points out that,

"E" has to go away now. It's all electronic. Because healthcare is now focusing on keeping people well rather than reacting to illness, we are focusing on factors outside the traditional walls. We have to knock the walls down whether they're the walls of the hospital or the walls of the clinic.

The idea of a CHR is to encompass "care that is not in the hospital but [which] has to be part of the picture." This would include

more types of data, such as social determinants, about what people eat, how much they sleep, if they are obese or live in a food desert (or both), and whether they are lonely, because all of those factors can have an enormous impact on an individual's health.

Epic has also been putting its money where its mouth is, taking a step toward EHR interoperability by offering an app called *Share Everywhere*, which is designed to allow patients to access their healthcare records on a mobile device or a computer, so they can show them to a doctor or a healthcare provider. It is not true interoperability, but it is a baby step toward it. It is also currently only available in California and at large medical centers. As Charles Christian, VP of technology and engagement at the Indiana Health Information Exchange, explained: "It's not really moving data around but providing access to it."

Faulkner's comments show that she is seeing sense and that she has got both eyes on the future of healthcare. Prevention is better than the cure, and by building more CHRs, we will be able to feed AIs with more data and arrive at more efficient and more value-based treatment options.

AI as the Paradigm Shift

I recently discovered a fascinating interview with Roy Smythe MD, who was appointed Chief Medical Officer of Healthcare Informatics at Philips in January 2017. Philips, of course, is one of the world's leading health technology companies, with a focus on improving patient outcomes "from healthy living and prevention to diagnosis, treatment and home care."

Philips has already been investing a sizeable chunk of its budget and attention in the burgeoning fields of health informatics, AI, and machine learning, but at the same time Smythe acknowledges that their goal

> is not to replace the clinician but make her more efficient and effective – to augment the clinician with actionable information. Artificial intelligence will allow clinicians to see what they may not usually see, using aggregated intelligence from billions of images that the system has "seen" before, as well as the rules it already knows and will create as it sees them, and it will do so much more quickly.

In fact, Philips is pushing AI and machine learning a step further, ushering in a paradigm shift by using predictive analytics to throw up warnings about things before they occur or to spot patterns that a human might miss. And, of course, the interesting thing about machine learning is that the more it learns, the better it gets, until it is able to draw conclusions that could never have been built straight into the algorithm's core programming.

If we are to create this paradigm shift and to store the data we have in the CHRs that Faulkner envisaged, we will need more data, which is where the next generation of wearable devices will come in. It is likely that data will be gathered both from healthcare companies and consumer technology companies, and these CHRs of the future will need to take that into consideration.

The good news is that if we get it right, we will have the power to transform healthcare for the better. Way back in 1964, in his book *The Structure of Scientific Revolutions*, Thomas Kuhn said "widespread adoption of AI will create paradigm shifts everywhere." He argued that paradigm shifts occur when we reach a crisis point and acknowledge that our previous way of doing things is no longer sufficient.

We are rapidly approaching that crisis point—and AI is not just *a solution*. It is the only solution. I am yet to discover a workable alternative that will allow us to store EHR data without using a prohibitive amount of manpower. And, the same goes not just for capturing the data, but also for analyzing it too.

AI for Personalized Medicine

AI could well be the most powerful tool we have in our arsenal as we push for a future in which personalized medicine becomes the new norm. As Dekel Taliaz explained in an article on LinkedIn, "When we decide on which is the right treatment to prescribe to an individual, genetics is one part of the equation – yet we must also understand the patient's environment and its role on our health."

Environmental factors are a hugely important element of contemporary healthcare, and yet, all too often, we fail to take them into consideration. That is a shame, because it is not like we are failing to generate the data—we are just storing it in disparate systems with no system to bring it all together and to understand what the latent data is actually telling us.

That is where AI comes in. It could help us to process all sorts of different data sources to create an overall picture of every individual patient. Taliaz argues that this is particularly true when it comes to mental health issues, because while many factors are genetic, many more are environmental.

"The search for a single gene responsible for major depressive disorder has given way to the understanding that depression is a complex disorder in which multiple gene variants, each having only a slight contribution to the disorder, are involved," Taliaz explains. This means that there is no magic bullet, and while medication, cognitive behavioral therapy (CBT), and ongoing counseling can help, a change in environmental factors could be just as effective. I mentioned in my last book *The Future of Healthcare* that moving from Chicago to Honolulu could be twice as effective as medication, thanks to the increase in warm weather. But, this is something that medical professionals do not often consider.

Taliaz says, "Just because we're genetically programmed a certain way, it doesn't mean our body will choose to run that genetic program." This applies to other diseases too, such as breast cancer or dementia. The problem is that no human being could ever understand the complex interplay of both these environmental factors and these genetic factors. But, AI could.

Woebot

Not many people realize that depression is the leading cause of disability worldwide, although we are all too aware of how easily it can kill. There is still so much that we do not know about it. In the future, perhaps our smartphones will be able to spot the signs of anxiety, depression, and other mental health issues before they become a problem, but in the meantime, we are stuck with the problem of how best to treat them.

One of the best ways to offer help to people with depression is to make sure they have someone to talk to. The problem is that therapy is expensive and cost-prohibitive. That is where apps like Woebot come in.

Woebot is an AI chat bot that aims to help patients using CBT. Now, you might think that expecting people with depression to benefit from talking to a robot is a little far-fetched, but it has been tested in a sample of real people with depression and anxiety and the data backed them up. In a trial in which one group of students spent two weeks chatting to Woebot and another group was directed to a National Institute of Mental Health e-book, the people in Woebot's group chatted with the bot almost every day and saw a significant reduction in their symptoms.

In fact, online CBT is just as effective as in-person CBT, but it can be carried out at a fraction of the cost. After all, as Alison Darcy, Woebot's designer, points out, "A premise of CBT is it's not the things that happen to us – it's how we react to them."

In many ways, this is reminiscent of Mabu, a robot healthcare buddy that was developed by Catalia Health to engage in daily conversations. It acts as a 24/7 personal nurse that is tailored to your personality and your treatment needs and which gathers information on your progress and sends it to your medical provider. It reminds users to take their medication and even tracks faces so that it can make eye contact for a more realistic experience.

Amazon Makes a Move

Amazon is making moves in the clinical decision support market and leaving big pharma to play catchup. It is a smart move by Amazon because it aligns perfectly with their overall business strategy of selling more and more goods while making shopping more convenient. It makes me wish that I was the CEO of a pharma company, or at least empowered to change their strategy to align with the changing times.

One example of Amazon's ambitions in the healthcare industry is the fact that it has started to sell software that mines patients' medical records and aims to find ways to improve treatments and to cut costs. The only real surprise here is that it took them so long to do it. After all, its rivals are already on the move. Apple has been in talks with the Department of Veterans Affairs in a bid to allow veterans to move their health records to their iPhones. Microsoft and Google are making moves in the healthcare industry, too.

Reporting on the development, *The Wall Street Journal* explained,

The healthcare application is the newest effort by Amazon to tap into the lucrative healthcare market. This year, Amazon paid $1 billion for an online pharmacy called PillPack Inc. to acquire the capability to ship prescription drugs. The retailer has also been trying to boost its sales of medical supplies by working with hospitals. In addition, Amazon is eyeing greater sales of medical supplies through an app, embedded in electronic medical records, that doctors can use to send links to products that patients would buy, according to people who developed the app and doctors who have used it.[2]

Amazon's application uses AI and deep learning to normalize data. For example, when there are misspellings, abbreviations, and even slang terms in the data, traditional algorithms would struggle to process them. "We're able to completely, automatically look inside medical language and identify patient details [including diagnoses, treatments, dosage and strengths] with incredibly high accuracy," explained Matt Wood, general manager of AI at Amazon Web Services.

Another interesting move from the tech giant and the undisputed king of ecommerce is the launch of Amazon Comprehend Medical,

---

[2] See: http://on.wsj.com/amazonsoftwaremining

which is powered by Amazon Web Services and which is designed to help people to "extract information from unstructured medical text accurately and quickly."

"Amazon Comprehend Medical is a natural language processing service," the company explains.

> [Using machine learning], you can quickly and accurately gather information, such as medical condition, medication, dosage, strength, and frequency from a variety of sources like doctors' notes, clinical trial reports, and patient health records. One of the most important ways to improve patient care and accelerate clinical research is by understanding and analyzing the insights and relationships that are "trapped" in free-form medical text, including hospital admission notes and a patient's medical history.[3]

The interesting thing here is that Amazon's offering is similar to what social networking sites and search engines offer when they release an application programming interface (API). This allows third-party developers to take advantage of Amazon's technology while creating their own solutions, which is good news for healthcare. Everybody wins: Amazon benefits because they make a small amount of money for each record that is processed, healthcare companies benefit because they do not have to develop their own full-scale solutions, and the patients benefit because they receive better, more effective healthcare.

The Problem with Watson

A lot of people have looked to IBM Watson as a solution to many of the ills of the modern healthcare system. The problem is that Watson was not marketed properly, and now people are surprised that it has not cured cancer. Watson was marketed as an expert system that will come in and immediately start solving medical problems. That has not been helped by all of the news stories and the hype going round.

---

[3]   See: http://amzn.to/comprehendmedical

That is the wrong way of looking at machine learning. The whole point of the technology is that it gets better over time as more and more data is provided. Yes, it will make mistakes along the way, but it will learn from them. It is not too dissimilar to what we do as human beings. The problem is that we humans are impatient and do not want to wait for machine learning algorithms to fail enough times to be able to provide some sort of useful insight.

The marketing of Watson as superior to humans in competitions and games has set it up to fail in other instances. Real life is not as simple as games are, and machine learning algorithms often have problems once the unpredictable variables of the real world start to come into play.

And, in the meantime, pitting man against machine in arbitrary tests to see who is better could ultimately turn out to be counterproductive. It is not humans and machines partnering for better outcomes, but humans and machines in a soccer match for our amusement when there is real work waiting to be done.

AI Applications in Healthcare

The healthcare industry is so big and complex that the potential applications for AI are almost infinite. We are talking about everything from better diagnoses to improved workflows and resource savings. This is especially important in today's world when our global healthcare systems are overstretched and underfunded. Many of the problems could be solved if only we could bring the data together and analyze it with AI and machine learning.

The problem is that much of our data is stored in silos, which means that we are only processing and understanding a fraction of what we could be looking at. And, to make matters worse, at the rate at which we are going, our ability to accumulate and store data is increasing at a much faster rate than our ability to analyze it. We need a solution, and fast. And, that is where AI comes in.

Roy Smythe MD, the Chief Medical Officer for Health Informatics at Philips Healthcare, explains,

What healthcare providers have is incredible data but very few insights. And what clinicians really want is insights to tell them what they really need to know. For example, among the 2,000 diabetics in their patient population, who are the 10 that they need to bring in for a different intervention? Those are insights that they need.[4]

Smythe suggests that there are four main ways that AI could be used within the healthcare industry.

Improve Operational Efficiency and Performance

AI is able to process huge amounts of data that no human being could ever hope to handle, helping healthcare professionals to optimize performance, drive productivity, and improve the use of resources.

Aiding Clinical Decision Support

Thanks to its ability to process these huge amounts of data, we can use population health data to build up a fuller picture of the best healthcare decisions to make for any given patient.

Enabling Population Health Management

Building on from the preceding point, AI will enable us to take advantage of a mixture of predictive analytics and machine learning to reduce public health risks, to save on healthcare costs and to take preventative action to head problems off at the pass.

Giving Healthcare Data Back to Patients

It is time for the age of interoperable data to come to an end and for the power to shift back into the hands of patients. Today's patients have come to expect a more personalized type of service with full control over their data. The healthcare industry has fallen behind other industries when it comes to the way that it handles and processes personal information.

---

[4] See: http://philips.to/datainsightsquote

The Healthcare Opportunity

When we talk about the opportunities for AI in healthcare, we are mostly talking about innovative new systems that are designed to augment the hard work that our well-trained clinicians are already doing. They can take some of the load off them by helping them with their paperwork while simultaneously allowing them to make decisions based on a mixture of historical data and predictive analytics.

It is able to do this because AI is the perfect technology to parse through huge amounts of data to identify patterns and latent insights that have so far been overlooked. I talk a lot about how AI will make physicians' lives easier by streamlining their workflows, but AI can also help patients to lead better, happier lives. It can even help with preventative healthcare, which is all about heading diseases and illnesses off at the pass before they become a problem.

Better still, because AI can process data at scale, it can outperform doctors when it comes to the ability to recognize diseases. Even the best physicians in the world can only evaluate a limited number of patients and patient scans in a single day. True, AI is also limited, but that limit is much higher than it is for a human and both software and hardware are continuing to evolve at a much more rapid rate than we humans, who reached our current stage of evolution, Homo sapiens, around 315,000 years ago.[5]

AI could also help us to deal with other problems, such as the lack of specialized physicians in remote or underprivileged areas. Suddenly, AI could help us to boost the reach of human physicians beyond just their ability to service the local area.

An example of this kind of technology in action comes to us via Optolexia, who build a dyslexia screening tool which uses a laptop, tablet, or desktop computer attached to an eye tracker to detect dyslexia in small children. While the patient is reading the text from the screen, the eye tracker projects an infrared pattern toward their face and then captures and analyzes reflections on the surface of the cornea. With this data in hand, the tool then applies a cloud-based machine learning algorithm to determine the likelihood that the patient has dyslexia.

---

[5] See: http://bit.ly/homosapiensevolution

One particularly exciting area of this innovative approach to medicine is the concept of building super accurate tools that can automate the detection of rare diseases. If these algorithms were applied by default, they could help to detect all sorts of diseases that most physicians are untrained on or unaware of, and they could do this simply by processing any scans and other tests that are added to a patient's files. But, only if we're able to enhance interoperability and to open up our medical records.

At the 2018 GeekWire Summit in Seattle, Harjinder Sandhu, the CEO and founder of SayKara, took to the stage to talk about AI and the future of healthcare. During his talk, he explained that the technology has only recently crossed over into the healthcare industry because of a lack of data. "In healthcare specifically," Sandhu said, "if you look back 20 years, virtually every medical record was on paper."

Sandhu was also joined by Michael Calhoun (CEO and cofounder of Mindshare Medical) and Anisha Sood (Partner at Echo Health Ventures). Sood pointed out that we are creating more data as a species than ever before, especially thanks to wearable devices and ever-evolving smartphone technology. And, it will fall to AI to decipher all of this data and to help us to derive actionable conclusions from what we see there.

In the meantime, all three speakers agreed on one thing: that AI will not be replacing human doctors any time soon. "It may happen eventually, for a lot of use cases," Sandhu explained. "It's not happening right now. So the way to go about it, if you're a startup in this space, is [to] find ways to add value to the doctors today."

AI for Mental Health

I recently chose to leave my role at Novartis to join Johnson and Johnson to head their global strategy and innovation in neuroscience. My role is to develop drugs and digital health strategies around severe depression and suicide reduction. My main focus is raising awareness around mental health issues and looking into how we can bring about change in the future. So, you could say that AI for mental health is a subject that is close to my heart.

Here in the United States, nearly 20 percent of the adults suffer from some form of mental illness. Suicide rates are the highest they have ever been, hundreds of people die every day of opioid abuse, and one in every eight Americans over the age of 12 takes a daily antidepressant. It is believed that just depression alone costs 210 billion U.S. dollars each year, with half of that coming from absenteeism and reduced productivity at work.[6]

At the same time, the country is dealing with a shortfall in psychiatrists and mental health specialists. In fact, almost 4 in 10 Americans live in an area that the federal government designates as having a shortage of mental health professionals. And, over 60 percent of U.S. counties do not have any psychiatrists at all.

The good news is that AI could be coming to help us. It can power chat bots and other tools that can help to treat people on mass at a lower cost. There is another advantage to using AI software, too. People lower their inhibitions because they know that they are not talking to another human being.

In an article for the *Harvard Business Review*, Parie Garg and Sam Glick explain,

> More broadly, AI's scale can be both a blessing and a curse. With AI, one poor programming choice carries the risk of harming millions of patients. Just as in drug development, we're going to need careful regulation to make sure that large-scale treatment protocols remain safe and effective. But as long as appropriate safeguards are in place, there are concrete signs that AI offers a powerful diagnostic and therapeutic tool in the battle against mental illness.[7]

The authors suggest four main ways that AI could help in the healthcare industry:

Making Humans Better

AI is at its best when it is helping to augment what humans are already doing. Instead of replacing them, it is going to make them better.

---

[6] See: http://bit.ly/depressionstatscwmh

[7] See: http://bit.ly/aimentalhealth

Anticipating Problems

The idea here is for AI to crunch data in a way that no human being could hope to achieve, identifying hidden risk factors and spotting early warning signs. If we get it right, AI could be a powerful tool when it comes to providing preventative healthcare.

DR Bots

AI-powered chat bots are already being used to provide counseling, as is the case with Stanford University's Woebot, which uses CBT to treat patients with no human input required.

The Next Generation

While we are already seeing a number of benefits from the use of AI in the medical industry, we are far from reaching its full potential. A great example of this is Ellie, a virtual therapist from The University of Southern California's Institute for Creative Technologies. Ellie can read people's body language and, therefore, tell when to nod approvingly or to smile at what people are saying.

Other Uses of AI in Healthcare

We have already touched on many of the different applications of AI in the healthcare industry, but there are still plenty more to come. For me, one of the most underappreciated uses of AI is its potential to streamline the content that we consume and the research that we read in particular.

I have spent a lot of time working with clinical trials, and so, I am more than used to the systematic review process and the guidelines that research has to go through before it is published. Still, there is so much new information coming out every day that it is difficult for physicians to stay up-to-date with the latest thinking. This is especially true when you consider that they spend the majority of their day just struggling to stay on top of their paperwork. Reading research is often the first thing to go when people are under too much pressure.

The good news is that this is something else that AI can help with, and, in fact, we are starting to see a surge of different AI-based platforms that are designed to filter out the irrelevant and to provide us with only the information that we are interested in. It is like having a human physician manually reading every review and then sharing only the ones that are the most relevant, except that AI software can do this in a matter of minutes and even run in real time.

Another of my interests is the concept of personalized medicine in which every single patient receives a treatment plan that is unique to them. Of course, this would require a huge amount of work if human beings were to create every care plan, but AI can create these plans in moments and then provide them to the physician for approval. Better still, AI could analyze every single data point that is stored in the patient's records, from their lab results and medical history to their symptoms and any hereditary risk factors. Then, it could cross-check against other patients in the database to see which treatment plans worked best for them.

When you schedule an operation in a modern hospital, it typically requires a dozen or more people in the same place at the same time. Scheduling can be a real problem in the healthcare industry, especially when you are dealing with shift workers and unexpected emergencies that can force rescheduling. But, AI can help us here too, by identifying the paths of least resistance when resources need to be reallocated or operations rescheduled. Through a mixture of the smart use of AI and intelligent human input, we can rethink the way that we schedule both routine and emergency work and hammer out some of the inefficiencies that cost us time that we do not have. Scheduling problems have plagued all industries since the time of Ford and Taylor. There is still no single best scheduling system, and none of our current AI systems can solve the problem. They can help it, but they cannot solve it.

And, of course, AI has the potential to ease physicians' workloads and to help with diagnoses. This is already happening, as is demonstrated by the innovative program at Tencent, which has the aim of teaching AI to spot Parkinson's in three minutes or less. Carried out in partnership with London's Medopad and Kings College Hospital, the AI was trained on existing footage of Parkinson's patients and is already showing a certain amount of potential. Dr. Wei Fan, the head of Tencent's Medical AI Lab, told Forbes,

> This technology can help promote early diagnosis of Parkinson's disease, screening, and daily evaluations of key functions. The goal of Tencent and Medopad's collaboration is to help expand the remit of AI-powered movement assessment from sport and exercise to medicine and to reduce the cost of motor function assessment.[8]

Google is doing great things with AI, too. For example, it now boasts an accuracy rate of 99 percent when detecting metastatic breast cancer. As Kyle Wiggers explains for VentureBeat,

> Metastatic tumors – cancerous cells which break away from their tissue of origin, travel through the body through the circulatory or lymph systems, and form new tumors in other parts of the body – are notoriously difficult to detect. That's one of the reasons that of the half a million deaths worldwide caused by breast cancer, an estimated 90 percent are the result of metastasis. In tests, [the algorithm] achieved an area under the receiver operating characteristic (AUC) – a measure of detection accuracy – of 99 percent. That's superior to human pathologists, who according to one recent assessment miss small metastases on individual slides as much as 62% of the time when under time constraints.[9]

Another interesting use case for AI comes to us from the field of wound care. Our current approach to measuring wounds is expensive and imprecise, as well as prone to human error. The problem is that if you cannot measure the wound precisely, then you cannot monitor the way it changes over time as it responds to treatment. "There's a black hole of data here," Yonatan Adiri, the CEO of Healthy.io, explains. "We know that measurements are non-repeatable. I can send you a body of articles

---

[8] See: http://bit.ly/tencentparkinsons
[9] See: http://bit.ly/googleaimetastases

that show that when three nurses measure the same wound they get [significantly] different results."[10]

The idea is that instead of using a still image, we would be able to take short videos of wounds and then run them through an algorithm that could take three-dimensional measurements. This would mean a more reliable (and more scientific) approach to wound management, allowing doctors to measure length, width, depth, and surface area of injuries.

Modernization

If nothing else, AI is all about modernization, taking existing ways of working and rethinking them through the smart application of technology. Of course, AI was modern as far back as the 1960s, it is just that now it has undergone another 60 years of development and upgrades.

A great example of this modernization is the way that AI is being used to rethink patient communication, ultimately providing more support and improving outcomes. Equadex has done just this by using an AI tool to facilitate conversations between people on the autism spectrum who are nonverbal or who have language difficulties and who struggle to communicate with their friends and family. Without AI, the default approach would require families to meet with an attendant who would use a physical binder carrying pictogram cards to encourage communication. Helpitco, the app solution that Equadex came up with, contains a whole database of pictograms and includes the ability for users to convert spoken text into a series of images. They also plan to expand the technology to help nonverbal children and adults with other underlying medical conditions such as Alzheimer's disease.

AI also powers chat bots, which are effectively an automated, modernized version of support that can work well as a first point of contact for simple questions. Even voice assistants could have their place in the hospitals of the future, providing signposting around buildings and even just helping surgeons to play music and to access information in the middle of lengthy operations.

[10]   See: http://bit.ly/reinventingwoundcare

Then, there are the benefits when it comes to manufacturing, and pharmaceutical companies are no different. Cloud-based systems can offer up real-time and predictive analytics that track every aspect of production and which can be accessed from any device with an Internet connection. Many of these systems also use AI to power proactive suggestions that are designed to streamline supply chains and production processes.

And then, there is maintenance and repairs. Even with all of the checklists in the world, human beings are fallible and often forget to carry out routine maintenance or simply do not have the time for it. AI is even being used by elevator manufacturers ThyssenKrupp to develop hundreds of error codes that tell maintenance teams exactly what maintenance needs to be carried out on any given elevator. This same technology could come in useful for bigger, multistory hospitals.

Perhaps most importantly of all, AI is great at filtering through huge amounts of data to identify the most relevant messages for any given use case. Pharmaceutical companies can tap into this and the huge amount of chatter that is posted on social networks to monitor the performance of their drugs after they have received FDA approval and gone on general sale. Any adverse effects can be noted and drugs can be continually evaluated to monitor their efficacy over time.

Rehabilitation

AI is not just about streamlining treatments and ironing out inefficiencies in the healthcare industry. It also has some exciting potential uses when it comes to rehabilitation, whether that is by powering chat bots that can help to take care of the elderly or whether that is by offering new types of software that are specifically designed for certain types of patients.

For example, *The Evening Standard* recently reported on a life-changing AI treatment in which AI was used to help a graphic designer with Parkinson's disease to draw again. At the age of 29 years, Emma Lawton was diagnosed with Parkinson's disease, and as her tremors grew more pronounced, she found it more and more difficult to do her work. "I was relying on colleagues to help with sketches," she explained, which was frustrating as a designer. I never thought it would be able to be fixed. I resigned myself to the fact that it wouldn't get better. After all, there had been no new medicines for years. I never expected to be able to draw again. It was a pretty mammoth task…to be able to write.[11]

As *The Evening Standard* explains, the existing treatment for Parkinson's focuses on replacing dopamine in the body, but it has not been updated for over 50 years and has become less and less effective over time. But, Emma was lucky enough to receive a new type of treatment spearheaded by a team of Microsoft scientists led by Dr. Haiyan Zhang.

Documented as part of the BBC's The Big Life Fix series, the treatment relied on a wrist-worn device that created small vibrations to balance out Emma's tremors and to steady her hand. "We stumbled on something that could help lots of people," she explained.

As soon as I started using it, it inspired my confidence to do anything I [wanted] to turn my hand to. I realized that there was so much more I could do. It made me realize I was in control of my own future and career.

The story has a happy ending, even though it is still an experimental treatment that is not ready for a large-scale rollout. The Microsoft Research team is continuing to test the device and to monitor its effectiveness on other patients, while Our Mobile Health has partnered with Parkinson's UK to create "a library of apps to manage symptoms."

And, as for Emma? She now works as the Project Lead for Apps and Devices at Parkinson's UK, helping to spearhead the development of new solutions for fellow sufferers. "There are over 40 symptoms of Parkinson's," she says.

So there's no one-size-fits-all treatment or individual. The apps help people to create their own toolkit, whether they need help

---

[11] See: http://bit.ly/aiparkinsons

sleeping, swallowing or rejigging their memory. They help to regulate symptoms, so the swallowing app is a timer that reminds users to swallow. It's simple, but effective.

These kinds of technology-based, non-invasive treatments will be vital for the future of healthcare, and it is AI that will power them. "One man felt he had to leave his job because he kept dribbling," Emma explains.

But this kind of app makes it really simple to manage those symptoms. AI for me is the future of healthcare. It's fascinating, and allows us to be superhuman, to hover above ourselves and see things from afar to help make intelligent decisions. In the future, I hope everything will feed together. So your smart-fridge will connect to your wearable tech, and warn you that what you ate last night may cause some cramping, and that if you aren't able to walk, you should avoid travelling. It allows us to master our condition.

CHAPTER 8

The Future of Artificial Intelligence

The best way to predict your future is to create it.
—*Abraham Lincoln*

Healthcare is not the only industry that stands to benefit from artificial intelligence (AI). According to the research from Microsoft,[1] healthcare is the third top industry vertical that is being targeted by AI developers, with manufacturing and professional services taking the top two spots. Hot on the heels of healthcare is financial services, technology, government, retail, and education. Most pundits agree that healthcare is one of the main industries that is ripe for AI disruption, and if the jobs market is anything to go by, people are starting to cotton on to it.

Take the case of Babylon Health, an AI startup that claims to be able to beat doctors in exams. The British startup recently announced that it would be investing 100 million U.S. dollars of its own money into hiring 500 new scientists to focus exclusively on AI and its applications in healthcare.[2] Its AI medical service is already embedded in Samsung phones in the United States, and the company has multiple contracts with the U.K.'s National Health Service (NHS). I find it particularly interesting to note that when Ali Parsa, the company's chief executive, was asked whether they would submit their AI research for peer review, he said that the model of waiting 18 months for submissions to be accepted for an academic journal is outdated. The paper has still been published, they just skipped the peer-review stage so that they could bring the product to market and start helping people.

[1] See: http://aka.ms/practiceplaybooks
[2] See: http://read.bi/babylonhiring

Even the British government is getting involved. It has been reported that five new AI centers are set to open in Leeds, Oxford, Coventry, Glasgow, and London as part of a 50 million pounds effort to improve patient treatment by bringing AI to the NHS. Greg Clark, the country's business, energy, and industrial strategy secretary, said,

> AI has the potential to revolutionize healthcare and improve lives for the better. The innovation at these new centers will help diagnose earlier to give people more options when it comes to their treatment, and make reporting more efficient, freeing up time for our much-admired NHS staff to spend on direct patient care.[3]

A Reality Check

There are four main challenges that new technologies need to overcome if they are to be successful in today's marketplace.

User Retention

Getting people to sign up to a service is one thing, but getting them to stick to it is quite another. In the same way that people pick New Year's resolutions that they later fail to stick to, people also set health goals and then forget to put the work in. The next generation of solutions needs to overcome this.

Credibility

It is difficult to convince people to try out virtual healthcare services because they are not always convinced of the credibility of these services when compared to traditional medicine.

Payment

Someone will have to pay for these new services, but who? About 77 percent of the digital health startup executives said that finding the right

---

[3]   See: http://dailym.ai/governmentaicenters

buyer was either moderately or extremely difficult. On top of that, people are not great at planning for the future, so patients are more willing to pay to treat a disease than they are to pay for prevention.

Clinical Workflow

All of the insights in the world will not do any good if we fail to make changes and to implement those insights as part of the clinical workflow. According to one report from Microsoft, "With only one exception, all large-scale remote monitoring trials in heart failure have failed, because they did not close the loop to treatment. There is no effective supporting system nor adequate buy-in to integrate data into the clinical workflow."

The Cure for Biased AI

Algorithmic bias is a huge problem for AI researchers, but help might finally be at hand. Scientists at Columbia and Lehigh Universities have created a way to *error-correct* complex AI networks, and the idea behind it is essentially to expose flaws by tricking AIs into making mistakes. Co-developer Suman Jana of Columbia University explained, "You can think of our testing process as reverse engineering the learning process to understand its logic."[4]

The interesting thing about this approach is that it relies on using computers to analyze computers. By repeating tests over and over again and slowly changing the input, it allows developers to gain an understanding of what might bias their AI and lead to it making poor decisions. It is not foolproof and is effectively a brute force, break everything approach, but the team's research has found that it is still better than random testing, and it can help to identify problems that we might not otherwise have been aware of.

Co-developer Kexin Pei from Columbia University says that Deep-Xplore, the software, has a bright future ahead of it. "We plan to keep improving DeepXplore to open the black box and make machine learning systems more reliable and transparent," he says. "As more decision-making

---

[4]   See: http://bit.ly/curingbiasedai

is turned over to machines, we need to make sure we can test their logic so that outcomes are accurate and fair."

According to TheNextWeb, who reported on the DeepXplore process, "Isolating and eliminating the biases that cause AI to reach conclusions that either endanger life or discriminate is one of the biggest challenges facing machine-learning developers."

It is a challenge, all right. Luckily, I believe that as a species, we are ready to rise to meet it.

How Humans and AI Can Coexist

I recently came across a fascinating LinkedIn article by Kai-Fu Lee, the CEO of Sinovation Ventures and the former President of Google China. Lee talked about an old friend of his who "wanted to do something more meaningful – to build a product that would serve the people that technology startups had often ignored."[5]

His solution was to design a product that would help the aged, which eventually became a large touchscreen on a stand beside elderly patients' beds. "On the screen were a few simple and practical apps connected to services that elderly people could use," Lee explains.

> Ordering food delivery, playing their favorite soap operas on the TV, calling their doctor and more. Older people often struggle to navigate the complexities of the internet or to manipulate the small buttons of a smartphone, so my friend made everything as simple as possible. All the apps required just a couple of clicks, and he even included a button that let the elderly users directly call up a customer-service agent to guide them through using their device.

Lee points out that in today's fast-paced world, with everyone both working and living longer, there are many adults both in China and in the rest of the world who are too busy to spend time acting as carers for their parents. His friend's device seemed like a perfect solution, until

---

[5]   See: http://bit.ly/kaifuleelinkedin

he discovered that the most commonly used function was the customer-service button, and by quite a large margin. "The company's customer-service representatives found themselves overwhelmed by a flood of incoming calls from the elderly," Lee explains. "Were his users still unable to navigate the one-click process onscreen?"

It turns out that the elderly patients could navigate the device without a problem. They were calling because they were lonely, and they wanted someone to talk to. "Once [their] material needs were taken care of," Lee says, "what these people wanted more than anything was true human contact, another person to trade stories with and relate to."

Lee continues to explain,

In that touchscreen device and that unmet desire for human contact, I saw the first sketches of a blueprint for coexistence between people and artificial intelligence. Yes, intelligent machines will increasingly be able to do our jobs and meet our material needs, disrupting industries and displacing workers in the process. But there remains one thing that only human beings are able to create and share with one another: love. It is in this uniquely human potential for growth, compassion and love where I see hope. I firmly believe we must forge a new synergy between artificial intelligence and the human heart, and look for ways to use the forthcoming material abundance generated by artificial intelligence to foster love and compassion in our societies.

I agree with Lee, which is why, the subtitle of my first book was *Humans and Machines Partnering for Better Outcomes*. I also think that while there is no shortage of exciting new technologies that are coming to disrupt the healthcare industry and to usher in an era of value-based health, it is the human touch that really makes a difference to patients, especially when they are suffering from chronic or terminal illnesses. If AI's only impact on the healthcare industry is to fix our broken electronic health records (EHRs) and to free up physicians' time to spend with patients, I will be happy. But, I think it has the potential to do much, much more than that.

"As we transition from the industrial age to the AI age," Lee says, we will need to move away from a mindset that equates work with life or treats humans as variables in a grand productivity optimization algorithm. Instead, we must move toward a new culture that values human love, service, and compassion more than ever before.

Now, I am not saying that most doctors do not have this culture. Indeed, I think this is the very reason why most physicians get into the profession in the first place. The problem that we have is that they are frequently overworked and underpaid, and in today's stressful modern workplace, perhaps it is no surprise that these attributes are often forgotten when doctors are up against quotas and deadlines.

AI Will Not Take Physicians' Jobs

"Robots will take our jobs," says Larry Elliot in *The Guardian*. "We'd better plan now, before it's too late."[6] Unfortunately for Mr. Elliot, I do not agree with him. There is a reason why *The Guardian* posted it as an opinion piece. It is factually incorrect.

One report from Gartner found that robots are here to give us a promotion instead of taking away jobs, with AI set to create 2.3 million jobs by 2020. Even when you consider the 1.8 million jobs that it is set to remove, that is still an overall increase of 500,000 jobs.[7] Meanwhile, *The Verge* has reported,

> Only 5% of the current occupations stand to be completely automated if today's cutting-edge technology is widely adopted, while in 60% of jobs, one third of activities will be automated. Quoting a US government commission from the 1960s on the same topic, McKinsey's researchers summarize: "technology destroys jobs, but not work." As an example, it examines the effect of the personal computer in the US since 1980, finding that they led to the creation of 18.5 million new jobs, even when accounting for jobs lost.[8]

---

[6] See: http://bit.ly/robotstakejobselliot
[7] See: http://cnb.cx/robotspromotion
[8] See: http://bit.ly/thevergeaiarticle

A great example of how these new jobs might work in practice comes to us from the most unlikely of places: a cafeteria in Japan, which has hired paralyzed people to control robot servers. The robots are controlled by 10 people with amyotrophic lateral sclerosis (ALS) and spinal cord injuries, who work from home to control the robots that communicate and handle objects. Reporting on the café, which is called Dawn ver. β, NextShark explained,

> Behind the OriHime-D is Ory, a startup that develops robotics for disabled people. The OriHime-D can also be used by people involved in childcare, nursing care or other activities that prevent them from leaving home or a certain location. "Even those who can't go out can work through this alter ego and have a role in society," Ory noted.[9]

It is also important to consider that certain industries are more vulnerable than others. The rise of self-driving cars, for example, could threaten the four million Americans who work in driving jobs, representing 2 percent of total employment.[10] When it comes to physicians, though, it is a little different. In my first book, *The Future of Healthcare: Humans and Machines Partnering for Better Outcomes*, I shared an excerpt of a Neil deGrasse Tyson monolog where he responded to a question about whether we should send robots into space instead of human astronauts. "Split the question into two parts," Tyson said.

> Are you only interested in scientific discovery? Send robots. It's cheaper. You don't have to bring them home. If you only care about science then there's no rational reason to send humans, really. But here's the catch. I've never seen a ticker tape parade for a robot. I've never seen a high school named after a robot. I never saw a kid read a book about a robot and say, gee, I wanna be that robot one day. There's value in human inspiration.[11]

---

[9] See: http://bit.ly/caferobots
[10] See: http://cnb.cx/selfdrivingcarjobs
[11] See: http://bit.ly/robotsorpeople

The same is true for physicians. Sure, robots might be better at carrying out specific operations or at carrying out monotonous tasks without tiring, but it is the human touch that makes all of the difference in a healthcare setting. Ask yourself how you would prefer to find out that you have a terminal disease. Would you rather be told by a chat bot, or would you rather be told by a kindly physician who is on hand to answer your questions and to guide you through what to expect in your final days?

Freeing up Time to Talk to Patients

Primary-care physicians are currently spending six hours per day entering data into EHR systems. This equates to them spending more time in front of a computer updating records than they do on face-to-face meetings with their patients.[12] On top of that, these EHRs are not delivering the value that they could do, meaning that physicians spend over half their time lining the pockets of EHR providers instead of adding value to patients.

The good news is that this state of affairs does not have to continue, and AI could be the answer to that. Through a combination of AI, machine learning, and natural language processing, we could automate much of the note-taking and record-keeping that are eating into physicians' time, freeing them up to spend more time in front of their patients.

In an ideal world, the widespread adoption of AI would be accompanied by decentralized health records, potentially powered by a blockchain. This would hand control of the data back over to patients and allow them to take greater control of their own healthcare. And, of course, decentralized data would make it much, much easier for us to monitor population health as a whole and to provide more personalized healthcare to every single patient on the planet.

The pessimists will tell you that it is never going to happen, or they will echo Larry Elliot and his *Guardian* piece. But, I prefer to be an optimist.

---

[12] See: http://bit.ly/ehrstatsphysicians

A New Type of Provider

According to Zayan Guedim in an article for EdgyLabs, "Medicine is constantly on the cusp of a deep and far-reaching cultural and technological revolution. Conventional medicine and its empirical approach to treatment is gradually giving way to a preventative and ultra-personalized approach to medicine."[13]

Apple, Google, and other technological companies are at the forefront of this change, and they could well spell the doom for traditional big pharma companies and medical research labs. Apple and Google are particularly interesting because they have been locking horns for years, most notably in the smartphone market, and now their rivalry is extending to healthcare. And, that is a good thing, because competition tends to lead to innovation, and innovation will help all of us to live longer, healthier lives.

If anyone is leading the way in the healthcare industry, it is Amazon. In fact, a recent report from Wells Fargo found that consumers are all for it, with half of U.S. adults saying that they would *probably* use Amazon Pharmacy if the company pursued it. According to *The Street*,

A new report from CNBC said Amazon is finalizing its pharmaceutical plan. Amazon recently expanded its Prime Now service in Japan to include drug and cosmetic sales and has also formed a Professional Health Care Program to regular the sale of medical supplies and equipment in the US.[14]

In other words, by the time that this book is released, we will probably already be buying our medication from Amazon. If it is an emergency, perhaps they will even deliver it by a drone.

But, Amazon is not the only big tech player to be making moves. Google already has a huge amount of data on each of its users, and it can cross-check common characteristics of certain individuals to make a good guess at which diagnosis is most likely. Their parent company, Alphabet,

---

[13]   See: http://bit.ly/edgylabsarticle
[14]   See: http://bit.ly/amazonwantsin

has created a number of subsidiaries such as Calico, which fights disease and aging by processing biological data, and Verily, which aims to develop innovative healthcare tools and platforms. They have even resurrected Google Glass for use in the healthcare industry, including with the use of a remote scribe.

Apple, meanwhile, can gather huge amounts of healthcare data through the combination of its Apple Watch and the iPhone. iOS 8 gave users a whole bunch of new features for monitoring their health, and the Apple Watch can even track abnormal heart activity, log health metrics during a workout, and automatically sense arrhythmia.

The best thing is that these devices are not used exclusively for healthcare. After all, there are not many people who would wear a healthcare device around the clock, especially when they do not feel ill and do not suffer from any pre-existing medical conditions. Unfortunately, preventative medicine relies on picking up on problems before they become a problem, so we would ideally need a wearable medical device that people are willing to use when they are at full health.

That is where Apple, Google, and other technological companies could have an edge over established healthcare. If the devices that they create can cater to lifestyle needs—if they can look good and have advanced functionality while adding value that does not focus on healthcare—then it makes them much more desirable. In the same way that nobody carries a DSLR camera around everywhere but everyone has a camera built into their phone, no one will wear a healthcare device—but everyone will wear the latest piece of hot technology, and if it gathers their healthcare data at the same time, then all the better.

In fact, established pharmaceutical companies feel so threatened that they have started to combat the big tech firms on their own terms. GlaxoSmithKline, Johnson and Johnson, and other pharma companies are actively recruiting tech specialists from Google and Microsoft. CNBC explained, "The goal is to hire engineers to help modernize the processes that big pharma uses to discover and develop new drugs."[15]

---

[15]   See: http://bit.ly/cnbcgsk

How AI Will Impact Healthcare

Throughout this book, we have investigated a number of different ways in which AI is set to impact healthcare, from freeing up physicians' time to crunching the numbers on overall population health. AI is likely to revolutionize the field so much that in 100 years, it will be almost unrecognizable.

In the meantime, we can still make predictions on what we are likely to see. While by no means exhaustive, here are just a few of the main ways in which AI is set to impact healthcare in the future, courtesy of the 2018 World Medical Innovation Forum (WMIF) on AI.[16]

Unifying Mind and Machine Through Brain–Computer Interfaces

AI-powered software could act as an interface between humans and machines without the needs for keyboards, mice, and monitors.

Developing the Next Generation of Radiology Tools

Experts predict that AI will soon power new radiology tools that no longer require physical tissue samples from biopsies, reducing complications and the risk of infection.

Expanding Access to Care in Underserved or Developing Regions

AI can match or outperform humans at certain diagnostic tasks, which makes them the perfect choice in remote areas where a qualified doctor might not be available.

Reducing the Burdens of Electronic Health Record Use

As discussed elsewhere in this book, AI and natural language processing can reduce the amount of time that physicians spend sitting in front of computers instead of in front of patients.

---

[16] See: http://bit.ly/aiwmifresearch

Containing the Risks of Antibiotic Resistance

"Electronic health record data can help to identify infection patterns and highlight patients at risk before they begin to show symptoms," explains the WMIF. "Leveraging machine learning and AI tools to drive these analytics can enhance their accuracy and create faster, more accurate alerts for healthcare providers."

Creating More Precise Analytics for Pathology Images

According to Jeffrey Golden, MD, Chairman of the Department of Pathology at BWH and professor of pathology at HMS,

> 70% of all decisions in healthcare are based on a pathology result. Somewhere between 70 and 75% of all the data in an EHR is from pathology results. So the more accurate we get, and the sooner we get to the right diagnosis, the better we're going to be. That's what digital pathology and AI has the opportunity to deliver.

Bringing Intelligence to Medical Devices and Machines

We are all already familiar with the idea of smartwatches, smart fridges, and smart televisions. AI could bring a similar revolution to our medical devices, updating antiquated systems and bringing them firmly into the digital age.

Advancing the Use of Immunotherapy for Cancer Treatment

At the moment, only a relatively small percentage of patients respond well to immunotherapy, and there is no easy way of telling which ones are likely to receive the benefits. AI and machine learning may soon be able to make better predictions than human doctors when it comes to whether or not immunotherapy is the best course of action.

Turning EHRs into Reliable Risk Predictors

This brings us on to the idea of predictive medicine, in which we use the data that we have on patients to predict whether illnesses are likely to be a problem, both for individuals and for populations as a whole. We will talk about this some more in the next chapter.

Monitoring Health Through Wearables and Other Devices

Now that everyone has a smartphone and more people are wearing fitness trackers, AI has a huge amount of potential to tap into the data. "There's a very good chance [wearable data will have a major impact]," explains Omar Arnaout, MD. "Because our care is very episodic and the data we collect is very coarse."

Making Smartphone Selfies into Powerful Diagnostic Tools

Selfies are no longer just for showing off to your friends and family. They can now detect everything from craniofacial abnormality to rare forms of cancer simply from a photograph, and even now, we are only in the early days.

Revolutionizing Clinical Decision-Making with Artificial Intelligence at the Bedside

This is the concept that we are talking about when we talk about a Netflix of healthcare in which physicians are provided with treatment suggestions based on what has worked well for other, similar patients. Physicians would still have the final say, but the technology and the data it uses would help them to do their jobs more efficiently.

The Future According to Venture Capitalists

Toward the end of 2018, *Fortune* published a fascinating article by Bob Kocher and Bryan Roberts, two venture capitalists with a particular interest in the field of healthcare and health technology.[17] I highly recommend giving the full article a read, but in the meantime, here is a summary of their 10 top predictions for the future of healthcare.

---

[17]   See: http://bit.ly/2019healthcarepredictions

More Payer Consolidation

Kocher and Roberts say, "Many smaller payers will struggle to retain national accounts as well as to compete against pure plays in the Medicare Advantage and Medicaid markets making them use their strong balance sheets to become acquirers."

Physician-Led ACOs Will Grow

Medicare's latest Accountable Care Organization (ACO) regulations favor doctor-led ACOs as opposed to hospital-led ACOs. "Doctors will quickly realize that they can earn much higher wages independent from hospitals," the authors predict. "Moreover, access to capital, managed care contracts, and low-cost analytical tools will make it easier for doctors to gain the benefits of scale while retaining independence."

Doctors Get Less Dissatisfied

The idea here is that healthcare leaders will realize that they cannot afford to replace doctors who threaten to retire or resign. They will be forced to take their concerns seriously and to invest time and money into improving the legacy systems that are the cause of much of the dissatisfaction.

Interoperability Becomes Interoperable

"Electronic health record firms are coalescing around standards for exchanging data (HL7 FHIR)," the authors say. "And CMS is expressing willingness to use regulatory power to drive adoption with the 'patients over paperwork' initiative." It is about time.

Consolidation in Digital Health

There has been an explosion of growth in the health-tech industry over the last 10 years, and the argument here is that it is time to sort the wheat from the chaff. As competition stiffens up, consolidation will become a necessity, as people struggle to survive.

Insuretech Takes a Lump or Two

"We think that we're near peak hype cycle for insurance technology," the authors say.

> 2019 is likely to be a year of toe stubbing for money. Start-up payers that have enjoyed great fundraising success are likely to find the very complex operation and scaling required for their actual business much harder than investor PowerPoint pitch creation.

Dialysis Disrupted

Here, the argument is that there is no need for patients to keep driving to brick-and-mortar dialysis centers three times a week. It is better for patients to have their blood cleaned daily, and it is also cheaper if they are able to do it at home. We can save money while simultaneously improving patient outcomes by providing home dialysis machines.

Telemedicine Takes Off

We have already seen the healthcare industry taking steps in this direction, but the authors believe that 2019 will finally be the year in which telemedicine goes mainstream and starts to be fully embraced by the general public. The authors expect telemedicine usage to double year-on-year.

PBM Disruption Talk Becomes Reality

"Drugs are marked-up, on average, 40% by the distribution system," the authors explain. "The current opacity about how money flows leads to patients paying more for drugs and excessively large margins being captured by intermediaries. We expect next generation pharmacy supply ecosystem efforts to gain real traction in 2019."

Real Progress with New DNA Sequencing Platforms

The field of DNA sequencing is a large, rapidly growing industry that has seen a particular spike over the last couple of years. The authors say,

We believe that new sequencing platforms (or at least the specter of them) will enter the fray in 2019, leading to decreasing per GB pricing (while still providing healthy margins) which will both open up additional application and volume as well as erode Illumina's market dominance.

Continuous Monitoring

Throughout my books so far, I have mostly focused on how the future of healthcare will impact the care of human beings, but veterinary care is also an interesting subset of the healthcare industry and many of the same technologies can be applied.

One of my favorite examples of this comes via Alexa Anthony, an NCAA champion on the equestrian team of the University of South Carolina. Her mother and her sister also work with horses, but Anthony has found herself becoming an unexpected entrepreneur after creating Magic AI, a Seattle-based company that has released a product called Stable-Guard—"the world's only artificially intelligent, 24-hour monitoring and alert system for horses."[18]

The idea behind a continuous monitoring system is simple, and in the case of StableGuard, it was inspired by a real-life tragedy. On Christmas night of 2012, Anthony's eight-year-old horse was stricken with colic. The digestive disorder can kill, but it can also be treated if it is caught early enough. "If this happens in the middle of the night when no one is watching," Anthony explains,

> they can go all night with this and in the morning oftentimes it's too late. That's what happened with my horse. But if there was something that had notified me as soon as he was showing symptoms of distress, I could have gone out there and given him a shot of benamine. We could have prevented it. He would probably still be here today.

---

[18]   See: http://bit.ly/aiforhorses

Now, if you are anything like me, you are already thinking about how this same technology can—and should—be rolled out to treat humans. After all, it is not just horses whose lives could be saved. I would like to talk to you about Lorrie McCombs.

Lorrie McCombs is a patient who died at Kennestone Hospital after being given opioids for pain without proper monitoring. McCombs was at risk of respiratory depression for a number of reasons, including chest and abdominal injuries, and the fact that she was morbidly obese. And, if she had been monitored with pulse oximetry and capnography—as is advocated by the ASA Standards for Basic Anesthetic Monitoring—there is no reason why she would not have been alive today.[19]

McCombs' widower was recently awarded more than 3.2 million U.S. dollars in a malpractice suit, but no amount of money can bring someone back from the dead. And, would it not have made more sense to spend that money on a continuous monitoring system so that the whole sad situation could have been avoided?

What is exciting to me is the fact that today's continuous monitoring systems already have the potential to save the lives of both animals and humans, and yet, we have not seen anything yet. As technology continues to develop, these systems will only get better and better, especially after we combine new sensor technologies with AI and machine learning. Imagine a monitoring system that is able to teach itself what to look out for.

The future might be closer than you think.

Healthcare 3.0

My good friend Zubin Damania, better known as ZDoggMd, recently gave a talk about Healthcare 3.0 while addressing the 30th annual Institute for Healthcare Improvement's National Forum. According to Fierce Healthcare,

> As Damania explains it, Health 1.0 built strong relationships between patients and doctors but was paternalistic and lacked the quality oversight the industry sees today. Health 2.0, where we are

---

[19] See: http://bit.ly/continuousmonitoringcase

now, moved the industry forward with new technology but was plagued with its own problems.[20]

Damania says,

> Electronic health records are the prime example – doctors were promised iPhones, but were given "1992 car phones." Health 2.0 is a story of failed potential and failed process. The future of healthcare will be a mashup of the old-school, personal approach and more modern technology and quality measurement.

Speaking at the National Forum event, Damania explained that the healthcare systems of the future will cater to the demands of both patients and providers. In our current system, patients and providers are at odds with each other, with patients being driven by emotion and impulse and providers being driven by logic and reasoning. He compares providers to riders on the back of elephants (the patients).

"The rider is often beholden to the whims of the elephant," Damania says.

> For example, a patient who's told it's time for a vaccination may go online and reject the vaccine because a celebrity believes they're linked to autism. The disconnect between these two also drives [physician burnout]. Doctors become caught up in the idea that they can't change the system, which is driven by their inner "elephant."

---

[20] See: http://bit.ly/zdogghealth30

CHAPTER 9

Implementing an AI Strategy

A vision without a strategy remains an illusion

—Lee Bolman

Congratulations

You are officially ready to take what you have learned about artificial intelligence (AI) and to put it into practice.

The goal of AI should be to take human ingenuity, attach a rocket to it, blending technology with ethics, accountability, and inclusive design to empower as many people as possible. AI should benefit society, not dehumanize it. That is why, it can help to think with a *humans-first* approach. If it is not adding value to humans, you have to ask yourself why the AI exists in the first place.

To get started, I recommend following this simple five-step process.

Define the Strategy

Identify what you hope to get from the use of AI and how you plan to implement it, as well as any resources that will be required along the way.

Recruit and Train

This stage involves hiring the staff you need to make your vision a reality while simultaneously training existing staff to take advantage of new systems.

Operationalize

Prepare to launch your new AI-based systems by making them a part of your operations. Ensure that all of the systems, tools, and processes are in place and understood by all employees before they go live.

Deployment

This is the stage at which your new AI-based systems go live and begin supporting physicians and serving patients. This is where all of the hard work starts to pay off and to deliver results.

Optimize

One of the main benefits of using digital technologies like AI is that they can provide metrics and analytics that are designed to help you to further improve your systems.

Define the Strategy

With this structure in place, you are ready to start developing your AI strategy. Remember that the strategy you work on now will form the foundations of the company that you will build. Developing the strategy is one of the most important things you can do, and so, do not be afraid to invest your time into it.

By now, you should have a good understanding of the opportunities that AI has to offer. The next step is to identify your focus, which is the technical way of saying that you need to find solutions that marry human ingenuity with the smart use of technology. Perhaps, you are helping customers to learn from imperfect data through the smart use of natural language processing. Perhaps, you are using AI to interpret text, voice, and images. The strategy that you develop will ultimately be informed by what you are trying to achieve.

Recruit and Train

When you are hiring staff and developing an AI team at your healthcare company, you need to consider what kind of talent you need. Tapping into existing APIs and using them to develop new healthcare-specific use cases is one thing. Developing complex custom modeling software is something else entirely. That is why, you will need to have a good idea of what is needed before you start inviting people for interviews. There is no point building a team if its expertise does not tie in with what you are trying to achieve.

Custom modeling often calls for machine learning solutions, which require a very specific set of skills. No, not like Liam Neeson from the *Taken* movie. We are talking about the ability to create machine learning algorithms and to understand data collection and analysis, as well as the rules and regulations that they are required to follow. Healthcare industry experience is always a plus because, like the finance industry, it is heavily regulated and bound to a different set of criteria than many other industries. Plus, industry expertise tends to lead to a better, more bespoke piece of software.

Operationalize

For most companies, the first step toward operationalizing their approach to AI comes in the form of bringing older, legacy applications up-to-date. That is because it is often easier to focus on one tool or one process at a time than it is to try to change too much too quickly. The problem with this is that the ultimate goal is to transform your business processes and to reach full maturity as an AI-based healthcare company.

Still, there are plenty of opportunities for AI in healthcare, as is evidenced by Tractica's 2017 Artificial Intelligence Market Forecasts report,[1] which listed patient data processing and medical image analysis among its top 10 use cases. The key to actually deploying these new AI-based systems is to make them a part of your operations and to provide training as appropriate so that everyone's ready to use them before they go live.

Deployment

To understand how AI models are deployed, you first need to understand how they are created. The goal of a model is to identify the relationships between input data and historical outcomes in such a way that it can start to draw conclusions.

For this to happen, the data must be gathered from its sources and prepared for the model. This may require a data specialist who can clean it up and remove any duplicates, a task which can take up to 80 percent

---

[1]   See: http://bit.ly/tracticareport

of the time required for the entire development and deployment process. With this complete, the model can be built, and a subset of the data can be fed into it. At this point, the model starts to evolve as it makes its predictions based upon the input and then evaluates how it performed. It can then *learn* to do more of what worked and less of what did not.

Once the model is ready to be rolled out, we enter the deployment stage. Here, the focus shifts from data scientists to developers, whose role it is to take the model file and to build it into a user interface that is easily accessible for end users.

Optimize

No model is complete once it has been deployed. Additional testing is always an option, and you can take what you learn from the tests to further optimize your AI software. On top of that, software can be upgraded or kitted out with new and improved functionality.

One example of this is Microsoft's Speech API, which uses AI to convert recordings of human speech into text. The problem is that while this might work well for conversational, everyday speech, it is going to struggle converting a doctor's notes into electronic health records (EHRs). Using the application programming interface (API) helps to keep costs low and to cut corners, but it is not necessarily the best solution for the long run. Better the API than nothing, though.

Another good example of optimization is moving your data to the cloud. When your data is hosted in the cloud, it can be accessed by any validated user on any compatible device, allowing staff to access real-time data in a much more convenient format. The cloud works particularly well with AI because you can upgrade your account and add resources as needed.

Building Your Team

When you are building a team of AI professionals, the first step is to identify the skills that they will need. Remember that there is a difference between building a new team from scratch and simply hiring to fill a few gaps. It is also not a problem if you end up with overlapping skillsets, as the goal is to continue to grow your AI division as more and more data becomes available.

Getting recruitment right is not easy, but following these three steps can make a big difference, especially when hiring AI and machine learning talent:

Define the Roles

You cannot start hiring people unless you know what roles you are looking to fill. Remember that these role definitions are not set in stone, and that people's jobs tend to change and to expand over time.

Identify Skill Gaps

Let us say that you have plenty of programmers and AI specialists, but that you are always struggling to clean your data. That would suggest that there is a skill gap, and that you should be looking into hiring a data scientist.

Train Your Team

By offering formal training programs and the ability to gain certifications, you encourage promotion from within. Sometimes, you can meet a skills shortage without needing to make a hire.

When it comes to defining the roles, it can help to know about some of the more common positions. Here are just a few of the roles that people typically look to fill when they are implementing an AI strategy.

Chief Data Officer

This high-ranking member of the C-Suite is responsible for all of the data that your company has access to. Their goal is ultimately to coordinate staff and to ensure that data is being stored in compliance with national and international law.

Data or AI Scientist

Responsible for creating models to solve problems and to discover insights. In the healthcare industry, this typically means identifying areas of potential improvement in conjunction with physicians and healthcare professionals.

Data Architect

These employees work alongside data scientists to take models and to prepare them for deployment. They specialize in designing the AI solution, managing the way that it stores and interacts with data, and providing guidance to data engineers and data developers.

Data Engineer

Data engineers work alongside data architects and provide the infrastructure that is required to make data accessible to other employees.

Data Developer

Responsible for coding user interfaces, implementing APIs, and creating more streamlined data collection systems.

My Process

There are as many different ways of approaching a technological rollout at a healthcare company, as there are different technologies for us to tap into. Every organization is different and what works at one will not necessarily work at another. Still, this simple four-step process has served me well in 80 percent of cases, and the chances are that it will work for you too:

#1: *Set the Scope:* Briefly describe the project, including high-level goals, the brands involved, and the data strategy. This scope will be used to inform the rest of the strategy, so be sure to spend some time getting it just right.

#2: *Consider the Data*: Create a list of all of the different types of data being collected, including demographic data, personally identifiable information, device data, and medical history. Then, identify how you plan to use that data and try to spot areas where you are either gathering data that you do not need or where you are not gathering data that will be vital for the future. This is also the stage at which you should identify how long you need to store the data for the purposes of the project.

#3: *Identify the Vendors*: Are there any vendors involved? If so, list out their names and state their roles when it comes to the data. Then, identify whether there are any contracts in place. If no contracts are in place, seek them out or look at sample contracts to identify what you might be getting into.

#4: *Think Global:* This is the stage at which you should identify which countries are involved in the project, as well as which organizations will be processing the data. If data is being shared outside of your company, identify who it is being shared with and in what countries.

If you follow these four steps, you should be in a good place when it comes to data compliance and your infrastructure. It is the process that I used during my time leading innovation and strategy in some of the world's largest pharmaceutical companies. If you are dealing with data, it will help you to get the job done without putting patients' information at risk or falling foul of international data protection laws.

Improving Buy-In

It is all well and good to say that AI has the potential to change the health-care industry for the better, but simply saying it is not always enough to get CEOs to take action. To get buy-in, you need to show them how AI can transform their business, which is one of the reasons why I wrote this book. Consider giving them a copy and encouraging them to read it.

For AI to achieve mainstream adoption across the healthcare industry, it must overcome the concerns of both the public and healthcare professionals. A survey by PwC and YouGov found that 47 percent of the British citizens would be willing to use an intelligent healthcare system via a smartphone, tablet, or personal computer. Unsurprisingly, the figure climbed among the younger generation.

However, the problem is that the metrics start to drop when the questions touch on more sensitive areas of healthcare, with 37 percent saying they would use AI to monitor a heart condition and just 3 percent saying they would use it to monitor pregnancy. This clearly shows that there is a lot of work to be done before AI tools gain widespread acceptance among the general public, but the report notes that as early adopters begin to use the technology, it will help people to become more accustomed to it and will eventually lead to full adoption.

Meanwhile, when it comes to healthcare professionals, the main concerns are around safety and efficacy, as well as the intuitiveness and user-friendliness of AI systems. "Including clinicians in the process of designing the interfaces they will use is extremely important," the authors explain. "Moreover, clinicians need some degree of transparency and interpretability over the results produced by AI systems to understand how the diagnostic, prognosis or treatment plan was reached."

Of course, many proprietary AI systems are so-called black box systems, which essentially means that they do not explain how they arrived at their results. It is a bit like plugging a sum into a calculator and receiving a result instead of *showing your working out*, as we used to have to do in math lessons at school. Another issue is that these systems need data to be able to function and to arrive at conclusions, but there is a "lack of public and patient engagement" when it comes to sharing data. This is another reason why we need buy-in from the general public, as well as from the healthcare industry.

It also does not help that public concern about privacy and data security is at an all-time high, boosted by a combination of new legislation like the EU's General Data Protection Regulations (GDPR) and a continuous string of high-profile data breaches.

"People's levels of reticence towards data sharing varies [depending upon the] type of organization the data is shared with," the report says.

> Commercial companies delivering health services are mistrusted by the public as they question their motivations. Nevertheless, over 60% would "rather that commercial research organizations have access to health data than society miss out on the benefits these companies could potentially create." The NHS and the industry must show patients that they can responsibly and securely use data to benefit the wider population.

Balancing Technology and the Human Touch

Andrew Ng, chief scientist at Baidu Research, says that, "AI is the new electricity."[2] And, he is not far wrong. I like this comparison because electricity on its own is useless at best. It is also dangerous: just look at

---

[2] See: http://bit.ly/andrewngelectricityquote

lightning strikes, which are a great example of electricity in action without human oversight.

When we think about electricity, we usually think about it in terms of light bulbs, television sets, smartphones, appliances, and other human inventions that blend a mixture of the core technology and human innovation. The same is true when it comes to AI. The technology is almost useless by itself. It is only when we blend technology and the human touch together that we get the best possible results. That partnership is what the future of healthcare is all about.

This human oversight is what will be needed to understand the insights that AI, machine learning, and other related technologies have to offer us. PokitDok highlights this by using the example of complex medical images, explaining,

> Consider these factors: numerous medical imaging devices in the market, thousands of observable imaging features, only 35,000 professionals in the United States trained to annotate, and the need for consensus annotations by multiple expert observers to minimize human error. This lack of granularity is a challenge even for unsupervised machine learning.[3]

PokitDok also points to Puneet Gupta of the Harvard Science Review who said, "Machine learning brings about a heated debate on ethics."[4] This debate largely centers around the question of whether—and to what extent—AI and machine learning will replace qualified physicians. The good news is that most forward-thinking healthcare professionals think that the future will bring clinical support tools that help to *lighten the load* on healthcare professionals. Lisa Suennen, managing director at GE Ventures, says that machine learning "allows clinicians to work at the highest level of their ability by making them far more informed and effective patient advocates."

"At some point, human judgement is a lot more valuable than any insights AI can provide," adds Kapila Ratnam of MedCityNews. The idea

---

[3]   See: http://bit.ly/implementingaihealth
[4]   See: http://bit.ly/puneetgupta

here is that as technology progresses, we will reach a point at which AI can flag the early onset of diseases before symptoms present themselves. It will then fall to physicians to decide whether to act or not. Ratnam also makes an interesting observation that I have not come across elsewhere, which is that it is often best to let the human body heal itself without medical intervention, especially for minor ailments and in the early days of diseases. It falls to human physicians to monitor the insights that AI delivers and to determine which actions are appropriate—and when it is best to sit back and to see how an illness develops.

CHAPTER 10

Predictive Medicine

Predicting rain doesn't count. Building arks does.

—*Warren Buffet*

The true benefits of artificial intelligence (AI), machine learning, natural language processing, robotics, and data will be seen when we move away from our current fee-for-service model of healthcare and toward preventative medicine. The idea is simple: instead of waiting for people to get sick and then trying to treat their symptoms, we can head illnesses off at the pass and stop them from becoming a problem in the first place. It might cost a little more up front, but it would save the healthcare industry a huge amount of money in the long run.

Predictive medicine and preventative medicine are similar but different, in that predictive medicine revolves around identifying what is likely to happen in the future, while preventative medicine involves taking active steps based upon these insights. Predictive medicine will naturally lead to preventative medicine, but it is predictive medicine I want to talk about right now because AI essentially relies on predictions derived from massive amounts of data. The more data that is fed into the algorithm, the better the predictions become.

Once we get into the business of predicting health, the industry will be forced to radically redefine itself. As new opportunities arise for health maintenance and prevention, so too will the number of services that are available to us.

There are different ways of approaching predictive medicine, from genomics and proteomics to cytomics and genetics. Genetic testing is arguably the most powerful way of identifying potential diseases decades prior to any symptoms developing. In some circumstances, it could even be used to identify potential diseases when babies are in the womb so that people who are more susceptible to disease can take preventative measures and modify their behaviors to avoid any risk factors. This is where predictive medicine becomes preventative medicine.

The overall aim of predictive medicine is to flag risk factors so that physicians and patients can work together to reduce the chances of future problems. For example, patients with a greater risk of heart attacks and irregularities could receive more regular electrocardiograms (EKGs) and cardiologist appointments. It is intended for both healthy people and for those with existing diseases, but the goal in both cases remains the same: to use predictions and preventative medicine to give people the best possible quality of life.

Precision Versus Prediction Versus Personalization

This seems like the perfect time to clear up any confusion around several similar—but distinctly different—healthcare terms. I am talking, of course, about precision medicine, predictive medicine, and personalized medicine. We will also take a quick look at patient participation, which ties the three fields together.

Let us get started with predictive medicine, which is what this chapter is all about. The idea behind predictive medicine is to identify the probability of illness and disease and to institute preventative measures to either stop it in its tracks or to reduce its impact as much as possible. For example, algorithms could predict patients' likelihood of suffering a heart attack and provide doctors with a list of high-risk patients so that they can suggest dietary changes and exercise routines. True predictive medicine uses a mixture of lifestyle data, demographic data, and genomic data to build a fuller profile on patients.

Personalized medicine is the natural next step for predictive medicine, because it relies on taking those predictions and then coupling them with customized healthcare treatments. The future of personalized medicine likely lies in clinical support tools that use machine learning to power bespoke recommendations in the same way that Netflix suggests shows based on what other, similar viewers have enjoyed by tapping into each different user's viewing history.

The precision model takes personalized medicine to the next step. Under a precision model, diagnostic testing is usually rolled out to help to select the most appropriate treatment options for specific patients, instead of simply prescribing whichever blanket treatment is being used for the patient population as a whole.

Then, there is the idea of patient participation, which is also known as shared decision-making. The idea here is that empowered patients can take control of their own health, with patients and physicians working together to make healthcare decisions. If patients understand what they need to do and why they need to do it, they are more likely to stick to treatment plans and ultimately to select the best possible course of action.

According to one article by Mother Healthcare,

> A general paradigm shift has occurred in which patients are more involved in medical decision-making than [ever] before. For example, a recent review of 115 patient participation studies found that the majority of respondents preferred to participate in medical decision-making in only 50% of studies prior to 2000, while 71% of studies after 2000 found a majority of respondents wanted to participate.

In other words, it is not just the medical industry that is calling for a shift to patient participation. The patients themselves are now starting to expect it as the new norm.

The idea of personalized medicine is nothing new. In fact, the process of tailoring medical treatments based upon the patient dates back to Hippocrates, and if you ask any surgeon then, they will tell you that surgery has always been personalized by its very nature—and that it always will be. The problem is that somewhere along the way, we took our eyes off the prize, probably due to ever-increasing budgetary and time constraints and the growing global population. Healthcare is no longer about that nice family doctor who always asks after the kids and dog. It is a multi-billion-dollar industry that is at serious risk of collapsing under its own weight.

The good news is that new technologies like AI and machine learning could be just what the doctor ordered, pun intended. There is a certain amount if irony in the fact that it could well be technology that brings the humanity back to the healthcare industry.

Precision Medicine

To give you a feel for what precision medicine looks like in action, I would like to point to the case of Teresa McKeown, who was profiled in a *National Geographic* article by Fran Smith.[1] Twelve years after McKeown beat breast cancer, the disease returned much more aggressively than before. Chemotherapy was ineffective, and McKeown spent her time sitting in a chair in her living room, keeping journals for her husband and her three children so that she could leave them behind after her death. The tumors in her bowel made it almost impossible for her to eat, and she ended up dropping to just 98lbs (44.5kg).

Before undergoing surgery to remove the tumor, McKeown said, "I'm so praying that if things aren't going to end well for me or if there's a complication following the surgery, that I just pretty quickly pass away. I don't know how much more pain I can tolerate."

Desperate for something to give her more time with her family, she asked her surgeon, Jason Sicklick, if he knew of anything that could help. She was lucky: Sicklick is a proponent of personalized medicine and was pioneering a new approach based on gene research and data analytics.

McKeown eventually joined I-PREDICT, a precision cancer study at the Moores Cancer Center. Razelle Kurzrock, an oncologist and the director of the Moores Center for Personalized Cancer Therapy, explained, "It's a very simple principle. You pick the right drugs for each patient based on the tumor profile, not based on a part of the body or based on what type of cancer 100 other people have. It's all about that patient sitting in front of me."

I-PREDICT ultimately matched McKeown with a checkpoint inhibitor called nivolumab, which has been approved for advanced melanoma, kidney cancer, and certain lung cancers, but not for breast cancer. When they went ahead and treated her with the inhibitor, the tumor markers in her blood dropped by over 75 percent after just two treatments. Four months later, tests showed no evidence of cancer.

---

[1]   See: http://on.natgeo.com/teresamckeown

And, 18 months after the treatment, Fran Smith caught up with McKeown, who told her,

> I just feel so grateful. I love this whole notion of individualized medicine. I love that they're figuring out what's causing that mutation and how to target it, as opposed to chemo that's so disruptive across the board. Can we just get there faster?

McKeown's story is far from unique, but it is also not yet the norm. Still, it is a great indicator of what the healthcare industry could look like in the not-too-distant future, and I hope that by including it here, it helps to add a human face to the subjects we have discussed throughout the rest of the book. When we are talking about patients, it can be easy to think in terms of numbers and figures and to forget that every patient is a human being with hopes and dreams and families that love them. We owe it to them to deliver the best healthcare possible.

Predictive Medicine Examples

There is no shortage of great examples of predictive medicine, and I have already shared many of them elsewhere in both this book and the last one. Here are just a few more to help you to wrap your head around some of the potential that predictive medicine has to offer.

Newborn Screening

Typically conducted shortly after birth, the goal is to identify potential genetic disorders as early as possible. This is currently one of the most widespread forms of predictive medicine, thanks to the U.S. state law that mandates taking blood samples of every newborn baby across every state.

Risk Testing

This approach to predictive medicine looks to see whether patients have risk factors that could exacerbate the likelihood of a disease. For example, a 50-year-old heavy smoker is more likely to suffer from lung cancer, emphysema, and other diseases than a 20-year-old non-smoker.

Diagnostic Testing

When a doctor has made a tentative diagnosis, diagnostic testing is used to confirm or refute the diagnosis. For example, a celiac disease blood test could be carried out to determine whether a patient is suffering from gluten intolerance or whether some other issue is the root cause of their symptoms.

Preconception Testing

The idea here is to test parents before they start trying to conceive a child to identify whether either (or both!) parents carry a gene mutation that could cause genetic disorders. Parents can then make a more educated decision on whether to try for a child or not, based on any potential risk factors.

Direct to Consumer Testing

This relatively new phenomenon is characterized by services like 23AndMe that allow people to test their genes with no need for a physician to act as a go-between. These tests may not be as comprehensive as other types of predictive medicine, but they do have the advantage of increased accessibility and greater privacy. Plus, they return power to the hands of the consumer, which in this case is the patient.

Prediction Machines

While I was carrying out my research for this book, I was fortunate enough to pick up a copy of *Prediction Machines: The Simple Economics of Artificial Intelligence* by Ajay Agrawal, Joshua Guns, and Avi Goldfarb.[2] I read a lot of books during my travels, often listening to them via audio book, but this one stands out as the best resource on the subject that I have come across. If you are already looking ahead to your next read after you finish this book, I can heartily recommend it. It is chock full of insights that can apply to any industry—but arguably to healthcare in particular.

---

[2] See: http://amzn.to/predictionmachines

Prediction machines will reduce uncertainty, but they may not totally eliminate it. Still, anything that gives physicians an edge could make a huge difference to our struggling healthcare industry. For example, the authors talk about what would happen if prediction machines were used to examine tumors. If they could give us a definitive answer of whether they were benign or not with no room for error, the doctor would find it easier to know whether to order an invasive procedure, such as a biopsy, to find out more. "Ordering a biopsy is the less risky decision," the authors explain.

> Yes, it is costly, but it can yield a more certain diagnosis. Seen in this light, the role of the prediction machine is to increase the doctor's confidence in not *cond*ucting a biopsy. Such non-invasive procedures are less costly, especially for the patient, they inform doctors about whether the patient can avoid an invasive exam, like a biopsy, and make them more confident in abstaining from treatments and further analysis.

Another great example is that of medical imaging, which the authors explain will need human oversight for the foreseeable future, although it is possible that AI will take over in the long term. "Imaging is costly, both in terms of time and in the potential health consequences of radiation exposure," the authors explain.

> For some imaging technologies, as the cost of imaging falls, the amount of imaging will increase. So it's possible that in the short and possibly medium terms, this increase will offset the decline in the human time spent with each image.

The authors also have some excellent advice on how to choose whether to use a specific AI tool in your business, which ties in with Chapter 9 on implementing an AI strategy. "Every task has a group of decisions at its heart," they explain.

And those decisions have some predictive element. We suggest taking those tasks and [breaking them down] into their constituent elements. Separate the parts of a decision into each of its elements. To see how this works, let's consider the startup Atomwise, which offers a prediction tool that aims to shorten the time involved in discovering promising pharmaceutical drug prospects. Millions of possible drug molecules might become drugs, but purchasing and testing each drug is time consuming and costly. How do drug companies determine which to test? They make educated guesses – or predictions – based on research that suggests which molecules are most likely to become effective drugs.

Atomwise CEO Abraham Heifets explains,

For a drug to work, it has to bind the diseased target, and it has to fail to bind proteins in your liver, your kidneys, your heart, your brain, and other things that are going to cause toxic side effects. It comes down to, stick to the things you want to stick to, fail to stick to the things you don't.

"If drug companies can predict binding affinity then they can identify which molecules are most likely to work," the authors explain.

Atomwise provides this prediction by offering an AI tool that makes the task of identifying potential drugs more efficient. The tool uses AI to predict the binding affinity of molecules so Atomwise can recommend to drug companies, in a ranked list, which molecules have the best binding affinity for a disease protein. For example, Atomwise might provide the top 20 molecules that have the highest binding affinity for the Ebola virus. Rather than just testing molecules one at a time, Atomwise's prediction machine can handle millions of possibilities. While the drug company still needs to test and verify candidates through a combination of human and machine judgements and actions, the Atomwise AI tool dramatically lowers the cost and accelerates the speed of the first task of finding those candidates.

The Problems with Predictive Medicine

Predictive medicine is not perfect, particularly now at this early stage. I prefer to think of myself as a realist instead of an optimist, which is one of the reasons why I acknowledge that there is a lot of work to be done before we can usher in the new dawn in healthcare that we are so close to—and yet so far away from.

One of the problems with predictive medicine is the risk of false positives. Even at a 99.9 percent accuracy rate, that is 1 in 1,000 people being subjected to the unnecessary stress and strain of thinking they are at risk of something that will never develop. Then, there is the fact that we may end up giving huge amounts of medication in a bid to prevent illnesses when many people might never have developed the disease in the first place. That would be wasteful, expensive, and inefficient, but there is worse. Many medications have unpleasant side effects that can reduce patients' quality of life.

There are also the ethical implications of predictive medicine. For example, what if employers start mandating genetic testing for every employee and if they use that data to determine who to invest in and to give promotions to? And, what if health insurers start to require people to take genetic tests before they will offer them coverage?

These are just a few of the ethical questions that we will have to think about, but the good news is that there may just be a precedent. Back on May 21, 2008, then-president George Bush signed the Genetic Information Nondiscrimination Act into law. According to KaiserNetwork.org,

> Under the bill, employers cannot make decisions about whether to hire potential employees or fire or promote employees based on the results of genetic tests. In addition, health insurers cannot deny coverage to potential members or charge higher premiums to members because of genetic test results. Supporters called the bill the "first major civil rights act of the 21st century" and said they hope it will encourage more people to participate in clinical research for treatments of specific genetic sequences.[3]

---

[3] See: http://bit.ly/geneticnondiscrimination

Diet as a Predictor

You may be wondering what diet has to do with the subject of AI, but it all comes down to the power of diet as a predictor. There is a reason why Ajay Agrawal, Avi Goldfarb, and Joshua Gans gave their book about AI the title of *Prediction Machines*. AI can help us to make better predictions about our healthcare, and it may well be our diet that provides some of the data that it relies on.

I recently came across a telling study by Kelly M Adams, Karen C Lindell, Martin Kohlmeier, and Steven H Zeisel on the status of nutrition education in medical schools, and it got me thinking about the role that our diets play when it comes to predictive medicine.[4]

According to the report,

> An overwhelming majority (88%) of instructors indicated that students at their medical schools need more nutrition instruction, whereas only 8% said that they did not. [Three quarters of this latter group] were at schools offering much more than the national average number of nutrition hours. The remaining 4% of schools responded that they did not know whether their students needed more nutrition instruction.

This lack of satisfaction with nutrition training is a major concern to me because our diets have a huge impact on our overall health. One of the reasons for the rapid growth of veganism over the last few years is that a whole-foods, plant-based diet is significantly healthier than a standard western diet. Registered dietician Cher Pastore says,

> Clinical research studies have shown that adopting a low-fat, plant-derived diet can aid in weight loss, improve insulin sensitivity, reduce blood sugar and cholesterol and reverse a type 2 diabetes diagnosis. Heart disease, the number one killer in the US, was found to be almost nonexistent in populations focused on plant-based diets.[5]

---

[4] See: http://bit.ly/nutritionmedication
[5] See: http://bit.ly/cherpastore

Dr. Michael Greger is an American author, physician, and the best-selling author of *How Now to Die: Discover the Foods Scientifically Proven to Prevent and Reverse Disease.*[6] He is a passionate advocate of a plant-based lifestyle, explaining,

> Ironically, the side effects of eating healthy can be not having to take drugs. We should all be eating fruits and vegetables as if our lives depend on it, because they do. We have the cure, yet hundreds of thousands of people continue to die.

Dr. Greger is also the founder of NutritionFacts.org, a non-profit that is dedicated to sharing the latest research in the field of medical nutrition. On the subject of lifespan, the site explains,

> Japan has the number one life expectancy of any nation while the US falls around 19th. A study recently suggested that eating a single serving of berries every day could add an extra year to our lifespan. The available evidence also suggests that eating nuts (specifically walnuts) and beans may extend our life. A plant-based diet overall is thought to be capable of reversing heart disease and, thus, extending the lifespan by almost 14 years. A study found that those eating one serving of fruits and vegetables a day died 19 months sooner than those eating five servings a day, a direct correlation between plant-based diets and lifespan. Just reducing the amount of meat one eats can increase lifespan.[7]

And yet, in the vast majority of cases, physicians would prefer to prescribe medication than to suggest dietary changes. Some physicians actively advise against a plant-based diet, regurgitating the common myth that vegans do not get enough protein (false) or vitamin B12 (occasionally true, but easily solved with supplements). But, can you blame them when they do not receive adequate nutritional training during medical school? I wonder how many physicians realize that processed meats are categorized

---

[6] See: http://amzn.to/hownottodiegreger

[7] See: http://bit.ly/nutritionlifespan

by the World Health Organization as a carcinogen in the same category as plutonium and tobacco. The BBC explains,

> Processed meat has been modified to either extend its shelf life or change the taste, and the main methods are smoking, curing, or adding salt or preservatives. Processed meat includes bacon, sausages, hot dogs, salami, corned beef, beef jerky and ham as well as canned meat and meat-based sauces. It is the chemicals involved in the processing which could be increasing the risk of cancer. High temperature cooking, such as on a barbeque, can also create carcinogenic chemicals.[8]

Going back to that report by Adams et al., the authors explain,

> Less than one-half of the surveyed medical schools (41%) provided the minimum of 25 hours of medical nutrition education. Compared with later recommendations of 37–44 hours, the percentage of schools meeting the recommendation falls below 20%. That means that roughly 60–80% of schools are teaching far less nutrition than is recommended. In addition, nutrition education typically occurs during the first two years of medical school when the basic sciences are being emphasized. Nutrition does not appear to get much emphasis during the clinical years when nutrition concepts and skills could be applied more directly to clinical problem-solving.

To me, this is like spending 99 percent of our time teaching medical students to carry out amputations and only 1 percent of our time teaching them to dress wounds and to treat infections to stop those amputations from happening in the first place. Worse still, we are not even heading in the right direction.

"Because the number of schools requiring a nutrition course and the overall number of hours of nutrition teaching has changed little over the past two decades," Adams et. al. explain,

---

[8]   See: http://bbc.in/processedmeatscancer

it is not surprising that most medical students continue to assess the time devoted to nutrition as inadequate. From our surveys, it seems that instructors are even more dissatisfied with the hours of nutrition in the curriculum than medical students are. Thus, it appears that we are producing a pool of physicians who feel largely unprepared to counsel their patients about nutrition and to make appropriate clinical decisions on nutrition-related issues. With the rising epidemic of obesity in the US population and the knowledge that prevention is more likely to be successful than treatment, it is clearly imperative to ensure that medical students are adequately prepared.

Putting Smart to Work

"Technologies like AI, cloud, blockchain and the Internet of Things (IoT) are changing the world," IBM says. "But only if they can be effectively trained, trusted and applied. Together with our clients, IBM is putting smart to work."

I came across this on a microsite that the company created to share some of the different industries that these new technologies are being used in.[9] The list includes agriculture, automotive, aviation, banking, environment, freight and logistics, government, healthcare, insurance, manufacturing, oil and gas, retail, telecom and media, and utilities. One highlighted example is Plastic Bank, which "uses IBM blockchain technology – tackling ocean plastic and global poverty with blockchain-based digital credits."

My question is, why is healthcare not on the list? Predictive maintenance helps airlines to keep planes flight-ready, while weather and in-flight data helps pilots to avoid turbulence. Why are we not doing the healthcare equivalent? It is time to put smart to work.

That involves thinking outside the box and coming up with new approaches to healthcare. A great example of this comes to us from Sameer K Berry, a gastroenterologist in training who is called for a *smart*

---

[9]   See: http://ibm.co/putsmarttowork

toilet to help us to track our health. "In my gastroenterology fellowship," he explains,

> I will treat diseases of the gut. I'd love to see the next generation of medical-technologists designing hardware with features to monitor and diagnose gastrointestinal disease. It's a hard problem for all sorts of reasons, but both doctors and patients could benefit if we figure out a way to stop flushing away some of our most vital health information.

Berry argues that the toilet is due for an upgrade. After all, there have been no significant improvements to our toilets for hundreds of years. "I see a big opportunity to apply these innovations in areas where patients feel a lot of stigma," Berry explains.

> And bowel habits is a big one. It's also arguably among the most impactful and actionable data. One of the major roadblocks for wearables is a drop-off in engagement. It quickly becomes cumbersome for people to charge a device, log data, and remember to carry a wearable around all day. But toilets are used every day and conveniently allow for passive and continuous monitoring of personal health data.[10]

I wanted to share that story here because just a couple of weeks before I came across it, I suggested it as an idea during a talk during the Ai4 Healthcare conference and the audience laughed it off. Well, here it is.

Predicting Patient Outcomes

Google may know when you are going to die. The good news is that we are not talking about some futuristic dystopian novel here. We are talking about recent trials in which researchers were able to show that the company's algorithms could predict everything from a patient's length of stay

---

[10]   See: http://cnb.cx/smarttoilets

and their time of discharge to their likelihood of mortality and their time of death.

Writing about it for Futurism, Victor Tangermann says,

> What can we do with this information, besides fear the inevitable? Hospitals could find new ways to prioritize patient care, adjust treatment plans, and catch medical emergencies before they even occur. It could also free up healthcare workers, who would no longer have to manipulate the data into a standardized, legible format.[11]

To achieve this, Google is using 46 billion data points of deidentified data on over 200,000 adults to predict the outcomes of hospital patients. Quartz writer Dave Gershgorn said,

> While the results have not been independently validated, Google claims vast improvements over traditional models used today for predicting medical outcomes. Its biggest claim is the ability to predict patient deaths 24-48 hours before current methods, which could allow time for doctors to administer live-saving procedures.[12]

Gershgorn also goes into further detail about how Google's system works. "The biggest challenge for AI researchers looking to train their algorithms on electronic health records," he says,

> is the vast, disparate, and poorly-labelled pieces of data contained in a patient's file. In addition to data points from tests, written notes have traditionally been difficult for automated systems to comprehend; each doctor and nurse writes differently and can take different styles of notes. To compensate for this, the Google approach relies on three complex deep neural networks that learn from all the data and work out which bits are most impactful to

---

[11] See: http://bit.ly/googleaideath

[12] See: http://bit.ly/googlepredictingoutcomes

final outcomes. After analyzing thousands of patients, the system identified which words and events associated closest with outcomes, and learned to pay less attention to what it determined to be extraneous data. Typically, AI scientists have to carefully tinker with how their system interprets the data after it's built, like which number of layers are needed to make the decision most accurately. In the research paper, the authors write that this was done automatically by a previous Google project called Vizier.

Another great example of predictive medicine comes to us from MIT, where researchers have been able to use Wi-Fi signals to detect the breathing and heart rate of people in a room. In one example, the technology was being used to monitor the health of a child as it slept in a cot. In another, it monitored two different people as they sat in a room. It can even detect these signals through walls.[13]

It is pretty easy to see how this technology could be beneficial. In the example with the child, it could be used to reduce instances of sudden infant death syndrome (SIDS) and even to act as an early warning sign of certain illnesses. In the latter example, hospital wards could monitor the health of all patients on a ward-by-ward basis, providing feedback to both physicians and the patients themselves. It could even flag potential warning signs from hospital visitors, predicting potential heart attacks and other issues. Imagine that—visiting a friend in hospital could end up saving your life.

Personalized Medicine

Personalized medicine and predictive medicine go hand in hand. After all, in order to make predictions, we need to treat patients on a case-by-case basis. It is difficult to make predictions when you are approaching healthcare with a one-size-fits-all approach instead of using personalized medicine to treat every patient differently.

Personalized medicine is often referred to as precision medicine and generally relies on tailoring prevention, diagnosis, and treatment to any

---

[13]   See: http://bit.ly/mitwifi

given patient's biochemical makeup and medical history. In an article about this phenomenon for *National Geographic*, Fran Smith cites the example of I-PREDICT, a precision cancer study at the Moores Cancer Center. "Researchers there don't rely on any particular therapy," Smith explains.

> Instead, they analyze the DNA in a patient's cancer cells. Using special algorithms, a computer then scours data on thousands of gene variants, hundreds of anticancer drugs, and millions of drug combinations to find the treatment that best targets the tumor's abnormalities. It may be a new immunotherapy, old-line chemotherapy, hormonal therapies, or drugs that aren't specifically approved for cancer. The distinctive mutations that fuel a person's cancer may be its undoing.[14]

Our current healthcare system is all about generic blanket recommendations that are designed to do as much good to as many people as possible, but which that not have the desired effect on any given individual. This made sense 50 years ago, when we did not have access to the technologies that we have access to today, but Smith points to new tools like superfast DNA sequencing, tissue engineering, cellular reprogramming, gene editing, and more.

"The science and technology soon will make it feasible to predict your risk of cancer, heart disease, and countless other ailments years before you get sick," she explains.

> Many experts say that a decade from now, a DNA profile will be part of everyone's medical record. Geisinger, a large health system in Pennsylvania and New Jersey, recently began offering genome sequencing as a routine part of preventive care, along with mammograms and colonoscopies.

Smith highlights the work of geneticist Michael Snyder, who directs Stanford University's Center for Genomics and Personalized Medicine.

---

[14] See: http://on.natgeo.com/personalizedmedicinenatgeo

For nearly 10 years, he has been tracking molecular and physiological markers in his body. Smith explains that he decided to become his own guinea pig because he did not think anyone else would stick with all of the tests and monitoring—a reasonable concern considering he has been working on the project for a decade.

"Four years ago, his sensors picked up an infection, through changes in his heart rate and blood oxygen level, before he felt sick," Smith explains.

> When he developed a fever, he suspected Lyme disease. By the time the standard test confirmed his hunch, he'd already finished a course of antibiotics. He also watched himself develop type 2 diabetes. His DNA had shown a predisposition, but he'd dismissed it because he was slim and had no family history of the disease. After a nasty viral infection, his glucose level shot up and stayed high, so he thought he might have diabetes. His doctor initially brushed off the possibility, as he had, but tests confirmed the disease.

Not everyone believes in this vision of the future of healthcare, but I believe it is inevitable. Smith points to the history of the home pregnancy test, which initially sparked a furor after the Food and Drug Administration (FDA) approved the first kit in 1976. Physicians insisted that women would get too emotional about the results, with one technologist calling for legislation to "limit the use of such potentially dangerous kits."

These outdated concerns seemed all too real at the time, but the world has moved on and they are no longer relevant. I believe that the same will happen when it comes to some of the concerns that people express about new technologies, whether we are talking about CRISPR and gene editing or whether we are talking about surgical robotics and the use of AI. Either way, we need to address those concerns if we are to get both the healthcare industry and the general public to buy into the future of healthcare and health delivery.

CHAPTER 11

The Future

You cannot escape the responsibility of tomorrow by evading it today.
—Abraham Lincoln

No one can predict the future with 100 percent accuracy. The world is a complex, dynamic place, with too many variables for anyone to fully wrap their head around. That does not mean that we cannot give it a go, though. We can look at past performance, analyze the early impact of new technologies, and rely on good old-fashioned common sense to get a good idea of what to expect.

With that in mind, I wanted to end this book with one final chapter on what I expect to see from the future of healthcare, building on what we have talked about throughout the rest of the book and investigating how it is likely to work in practice in genuine healthcare settings in the decades and centuries to come.

Some of the insights here are my own, while others have been shared by other forward-thinking health professionals and summarized for your convenience. The truth is that every healthcare professional has their own vision of what the future should look like, and many of them are mutually exclusive. The future will be what we make of it, and it is too early to tell whether the healthcare industry is ready to face the sea of change that is in store for it. That makes it an exciting time to be alive, but it also means that we have a responsibility to future generations if we want to make predictive medicine a reality.

But, before we take a look at some visions of the future from today, let us head all of the way back to the 1930s.

Introducing FE Smith

It is difficult to predict the future without first taking a look at the past. We are going to take that a step further by examining a vision of the future from the past, courtesy of former cabinet minister and lawyer FE Smith, who was a friend of Winston Churchill. Shortly before he died in 1930, he wrote a book called *The World in 2030 AD*, in which he shared some predictions of what the world would look like in 100 years' time.[1]

To understand Smith's views on healthcare and lifespan, it is important to remember that he was writing at a time at which tuberculosis was one of the leading causes of death both in the United Kingdom and around the world. According to the BBC, "[Smith] was optimistic enough to suggest [that] the eradication of [tuberculosis] and other epidemic diseases was 'fairly certain' by 2030, as was 'the discovery of cures for such scourges as cancer.'"[2]

Smith also believed that we would live longer, with scientists creating *rejuvenation* injections that could prolong our average lifespan to up to 150 years. However, the BBC explains,

[He] acknowledged this would present "grave problems" from an "immense increase in population." He also foresaw extreme inter-generational inequality, wondering "how will youths of 20 be able to compete in the professions or business against vigorous men still in their prime at 120, with a century of experience on which to draw?"

So, it seems clear that while Smith got some things right, he was drastically off the mark with others. A great example of this is his prediction that cars would be obsolete by 2030 because we would all own private airplanes. "The man of 2030 will set off for the weekend, after his work, in a small, swift airplane, as reliable and cheap as the motor-car on which we depend today." Other predictions were more realistic. Bearing in mind that he died 40 years before the moon landing, he was surprisingly accurate with his prediction that by 2030, the first preparations for a manned mission to Mars would be underway. Unfortunately, the BBC also says that he thought "the first 'half a dozen' attempts could miss the planet

---

[1] See: http://bit.ly/theworldin2030
[2] See: http://bbc.in/fesmithbbc

entirely, leaving astronauts to die onboard as they drifted further from Earth." Someone should warn Elon Musk.

Other seemingly outlandish predictions include the survival of the British Empire, although he did suggest that the capital might shift from London to somewhere in Canada or Australia. He was also skeptical about renewable energy, predicting, "By [harnessing] tidal energy to any large extent, we should diminish the speed of the earth's rotation. [If it's overused], a 48-hour day is a possibility in the far future."

Smith also predicted an increased usage of eugenics, a branch of science that has lost favor in recent years because of its association with the Nazi party and their atrocities during the Second World War. Smith never lived to see that, and so, perhaps, he would have changed his mind. The idea is to *improve* the human race by controlling reproduction and ultimately artificially shaping evolution. The BBC says,

> He claimed a clever young man would "consider his fiancé's hereditary complexion before proposing marriage." In return, "the young woman of that day will refuse him because he has inherited a gene from his father which will predispose their children to quarrelsomeness."

Finally, Smith had a few ideas when it comes to food and pharmaceuticals, including the idea of synthetic food from laboratories overtaking conventional agriculture in order to cater to the growing population. He said, "From one 'parent' steak of choice tenderness, it will be possible to grow as large and juicy a steak as can be desired." If this sounds familiar, the chances are that you have heard about recent advances in lab-grown meat, which supporters argue will reduce concerns about animal cruelty while simultaneously reducing the impact that animal agriculture has on the environment.

And, as for pharmaceuticals, Smith wrote,

> Should chemistry in the next hundred years be able to discover new substances as pleasant and harmless as tobacco, yet each possessing a different effect on the consumer, it will have earned the thanks of every hard-worked man and woman in the world.

It is ironic, really, considering he died at the age of 58 after a lifetime of heavy drinking and smoking.

Smith's vision of the future is both surprisingly prescient and as wacky as they come, but I wanted to include it here for a reason. It is an important reminder in a chapter like this that predicting the future is a fool's game, and one that it is almost impossible to win. This is especially true when those visions stretch so far into the future that there is no chance of living to see whether the predictions pan out.

No predictions of the future can ever be 100% accurate. Nevertheless, that is no excuse to avoid thinking about the future at all; it is just a reminder that we should take those predictions with a pinch of salt. And, with that in mind, let us take a look at what the future might bring—personal airplanes not included.

Seven Visions of the Future

It seems like everyone has a vision for the future of healthcare, but not all opinions are born equal. I like to think I am more qualified than most because my career is built on the idea of ushering in the future of healthcare. I spend a decent chunk of my time familiarizing myself with the latest trends in the healthcare industry, and then, I spend the rest of the time trying to harness those technologies and to make my own personal vision a reality. I will talk a little bit more about my vision at the end of this chapter.

With that said, *The Telegraph* did a pretty good job of finding some of the key players in the healthcare industry and getting to know their predictions in an article that they released in partnership with Philips.[3] In it, they shared seven visions by seven healthcare professionals, which I would like to summarize for you here:

Jeroen Tas

Tas is the chief executive of connected care and health informatics at Philips, and he predicts a future where doctors and patients are connected. He says,

---

[3]   See: http://bit.ly/healthvisions

We've got to start looking at healthcare from the perspective of the patient. That is first to help the patient understand the drivers that impact their chronic condition better so they can play a more active role in managing it. This could be getting involved in health rather than just sickness, supporting and coaching them in relation to their sleeping, eating, smoking, drinking and exercise as well as all aspects of managing their condition properly, such as adherence to medication. The aim is to proactively keep them well rather than to react when they become ill.

In other words, he is advocating preventative medicine.

Professor Metin Avkiran

Professor Avkiran is associate medical director at the British Heart Foundation, and he believes in a future where heart disease can be prevented in whole new ways. Sound familiar? Avkiran is an advocate of both predictive and preventative medicine, explaining,

One area of exciting research is the identification of the casual genetic risk-factors that lead to some people developing cardiovascular disease. Another area of research is finding the drugs and therapies to target the newly discovered mechanisms that cause the disease. In the future, [we'll also identify] new types of biomarkers (chemical entities that can be measured in biological samples such as blood and urine) to indicate an increased risk or the early onset of cardiovascular disease. Improved imaging is moving at a rapid pace too.

Sebastian Conran

Conran is a leading consumer product designer and the co-founder of Consequential Robotics, and he believes in a future where robots help the aged to live more independently. He points to the emerging healthcare robotics market in Japan, explaining, "[They've] developed robots that can lift patients out of bed and move them from one room to another.

At the moment, these are expensive and operate via remote control, not autonomously." One of the key obstacles that we need to overcome is designing an autonomous dexterous hand and arm that can carry out multiple tasks.

Professor John Moore-Gillon

Moore-Gillon is an honorary medical advisor for the British Lung Foundation, and he envisions a future where asthma and some lung cancers are a thing of the past. "I believe in 10 to 15 years, although probably even sooner, there will be an effective vaccine for asthma," Moore-Gillon says.

> Although it will be hugely expensive to develop, it will be worth it as huge numbers will benefit. In 20 years, if not sooner, our treatment and management plans for those with chronic respiratory disease will no longer be worked out by doctors. Instead, patients will be monitored remotely and an algorithm will keep [track] of their health rather than a doctor.

Sonia Trigueros

Trigueros is a nano bio-systems group leader at Oxford University and the former co-director of the OMS Institute of Nanomedicine. She believes in a future where nano-medicines can cure blindness and even cancer, explaining,

> Nanotechnology has the potential to transform current chemotherapy treatments, with nanostructures loaded with chemotherapy drugs able to selectively target cancer cells, giving the benefits of chemotherapy without the side effects. Because of the complexity of the field of nanotechnology, and the need for clinical trials to prove the efficacy and safety of these new therapies, I imagine it will be between 5 to 10 years before nanomedicines become available. But there is no doubt that nanotechnology has the potential to revolutionize healthcare in the future.

Dr. Emily Burns

Dr. Burns is a research communications manager at Diabetes UK, and she believes in a future where diabetes has been cured. She says that new developments like artificial pancreases are being developed to treat Type 1 diabetes, while Type 2 diabetes can be managed with preventative medicine and lifestyle management if the disease develops. She says, "Researchers are also looking at a potential cure for diabetes. They're looking at the beta cells, which are the cells in the pancreas that the immune system attacks." We can replace those cells using an islet transplant, but they rely on donated pancreases, which aren't easily come by. Longer term, we're looking at stem-cell therapy. Here, we could make beta cells from scratch in the lab, doing away with pancreas donations.

Professor Peter Johnson

Johnson is chief clinician at Cancer Research UK, and his vision is of a future where three in four people with cancer will beat it. "I can see that individual treatment or 'personalized medicine' will progress," he says.

> As we find out more about the particular genetic makeup of tumors, we'll be able to give specific drugs to target it. In the past 40 years, the likelihood of surviving cancer has improved from one in four to one in two. In the next 20 years, we at the charity want to reduce that risk even further to three in four. I think that's a realistic aim as we're now at a very exciting time for research into all types of cancer.

The NHS Looks to the Future

Toward the tail end of 2018, U.K.'s National Health Service (NHS) published an illuminating report called *The Future of Healthcare: Our Vision for Digital, Data and Technology in Health and Care*.[4] They quite rightly explain,

---

[4]   See: http://bit.ly/nhsfuturehealthcare

The UK has the chance to lead the world on healthtech. We already have some of the world's leading healthtech companies bringing new innovations and advancing the international reputation of our excellent science and research base. And, in the NHS, we have the world's biggest health institution. We have the opportunity to build an ecosystem that continually creates the best healthtech – technology that can be exported, alongside new methods and insights that can contribute to health outcomes globally.

The NHS is not perfect—far from it, in fact—but neither is our system here in the United States. In fact, you could argue that the global healthcare industry as a whole is lucky to have the two different approaches of public and private sectors because it can help to foster innovation. The NHS can learn from the United States, and the United States can learn from the NHS.

Even the NHS itself is quick to acknowledge its own shortcomings, explaining,

The state of online services, basic IT and clinical tools in health and care is far behind where it needs to be. Technology systems used daily across hospitals, GP surgeries, care homes, pharmacies and community care facilities don't talk to each other, fail frequently and do not follow modern cybersecurity practices. As a result, some people are getting suboptimal care, [healthcare practitioners] are frustrated and money could be saved and released for the front line.

If the NHS—a centralized, public agency—is struggling to create interoperable systems, you can imagine how much of a challenge we face here in the United States, where different data is owned and stored by different providers.

"The gap between where we are and where we want to be is only getting bigger," the report states. "We need to take a radical new approach to technology across the system and stop the narrative that it's too difficult to do it right in health and care."

The NHS is also aware of the challenges, which include legacy technology and commercial arrangements, complex organizational and delivery structures, a risk-averse culture, limited resources to invest, and a critical need to build and maintain public trust. To achieve their vision, they plan to focus on four guiding principles: user need, privacy and security, interoperability, and openness and inclusion. "[We also] need to draw on emerging thinking on designing technology safely, ethically and effectively for the values and interests of civil society," the authors conclude.

It is interesting to see that the NHS is taking steps in this direction, and I am looking forward to seeing whether they are able to deliver on the vision that they outline in the report. Who knows? There might even be learnings that we here in the United States can apply to our own healthcare system. Only time will tell.

The Future of Pharmaceuticals

While working on this book, I was lucky enough to be invited to contribute to PharmaBoardroom, a healthcare site that provides industry trends, news, and reports from all over the world. As 2018 turned into 2019, I was asked to write a piece predicting the future of the pharmaceutical industry, and it got me thinking.

The pharmaceutical industry is ripe for disruption. After all, it has not really changed for over half a century, despite the fact that the Internet and the World Wide Web have revolutionized almost every other major industry on the planet.

To understand the future of the pharmaceutical industry, we first need to understand the present. The good news is that Ingrid Torjesen has us covered in an article that she wrote for *The Pharmaceutical Journey*, where she explains,

> Before a drug is deemed suitable for patients, it has to go through rigorous testing and cost-effectiveness analyses. Each year sees a couple of dozen new drugs licensed for use, but in their wake there will be tens of thousands of candidate drugs that fell by the wayside. The research and development journey of those new

drugs that make it to market will have taken around 12 years and cost around £1.15bn.[5]

The drug development journey begins when researchers undertake research to understand the processes behind a disease. This often involves identifying a gene or a protein that is instrumental to the disease and then searching for a molecule or a compound that acts on the target. "As many as 10,000 compounds may be considered and whittled down to just 10 to 20 that could theoretically interfere with the disease process," Torjesen says.

From there, we move on to pre-clinical testing and, then, clinical trials, usually consisting of phase 1, phase 2, and phase 3 trials. Each of these phases helps to weed out ineffective or unsafe drugs before they even get to the stage at which they are submitted to The Medicines and Healthcare products Regulatory Agency (MHRA) (in the United Kingdom) or the Food and Drug Administration (FDA) (in the United States) in an attempt to get a license to market the drug. "If a license is granted, that's not the end of the process," Torjesen explains.

> In England and Wales, drug companies need more than a marketing authorization for most patients to be able to access treatment on the NHS – they also need the National Institute of Health and Care Excellence (NICE) to recommend that it should be made available through the NHS.

From there, we move on to patenting and eventually a general release, but it is these early steps I want to focus on today. That is because a little thing called artificial intelligence (AI) has the potential to dramatically streamline the drug discovery process.

AI is great at processing huge amounts of data and arriving at conclusions, especially when it is coupled with its sister technology, machine learning. It can also be used to power complex simulations that emulate real-world scenarios and give researchers a good idea of

---

[5] See: http://bit.ly/drugdevelopmentjourney

where to focus their efforts before they even get started. It can stream-line the development process and save money, reducing a drug's time to market while simultaneously cutting any risks involved in the clinical trial stage.

Let us revisit the existing model of drug development. AI can help out right at the start by crunching the numbers and helping researchers to identify genes and proteins, as well as compounds that could potentially have an effect on them. It effectively points researchers in the right direc-tion, acting a little bit like a satnav. It might not get it right every time, but that is why, it will be supervised by human oversight. In the same way that you would not follow your satnav if it told you to drive into the sea, researchers will be able to take the AI's findings with a pinch of salt and to overrule it when needed.

AI will also be able to simulate clinical trials and even what might happen if there was a real-world release and if the drug made its way into the hands of the general public. This would not replace traditional phase 1, phase 2, and phase 3 clinical trials, but it could save pharmaceutical companies money by stopping them from investing in clinical trials that are doomed to failure before they even start. These savings—as well as the inherent savings from faster, more streamlined research processes—could help to keep overheads down and ultimately allow pharmaceutical com-panies to sell drugs at lower prices. After all, there will be less of an overall investment for them to recoup.

The future of pharmaceuticals is not just about AI and machine learn-ing. For example, blockchain technology has a lot of potential when it comes to data storage and transmission, while wearable devices could have an impact by helping patients to take control of their health and reducing the need for pharmaceuticals in the first place. I would not be surprised if Pfizer, Johnson & Johnson, and other major pharmaceutical companies switch their focus to more of a preventative model in which they become software and hardware developers as well as being traditional drug companies.

But it is AI that has the greatest amount of potential to bring disrup-tion, at least in my eyes. And, this holds true not only for pharmaceuti-cals, but also for the healthcare industry as a whole, and 2019 is just the beginning.

The Future of Health Insurance

Writing in a study for the *Annals of Family Medicine*, Richard A. Young and Jennifer E. DeVoe predicted that the cost of a family health insurance premium would equal the median household income by the year 2033. Perhaps, most startling of all is the fact that these figures do not include taxes paid every year to finance Medicare and Medicaid, so the true cost to the American public is even higher. The authors explain, "Private health insurance will become increasingly unaffordable to low-to-middle-income Americans unless major changes are made to the US healthcare system."[6]

It is interesting to note that back in 2010, we witnessed the passage of the Patient Protection and Affordable Care Act (PPACA) in the same year that the number of Americans without health insurance rose to a historic high of 50.7 million people after five million Americans lost employment-based health insurance in the recession. "It's ironic that uninsurance rates rose on the heels of the PPACA, which was intended to reduce the numbers of uninsured," the authors say.

"The healthcare system is complex and adaptive," they continue,

> so it is possible that other changes will occur to avoid a complete meltdown of the system. Increased cost sharing might change some patient expectations and behaviors. Empowering consumers to choose (and pay for) services might also increase price transparency, especially for expensive non-emergent services, such as outpatient magnetic resonance imaging. Healthcare consumerism has limits, however, because one cannot shop around for surgeons and hospitals when one has appendicitis.

As for the future, Young and DeVoe are not optimistic,

> None of the efforts to tweak healthcare costs using payment changes has bent the cost curve during the last 50 years. America needs a deeper discussion of the very role and importance of

---

6   See: http://bit.ly/healthinsuranceprojection

the healthcare system in our lives, possibly including new expectations of the doctor-patient relationship. Alternatively, we can choose to continue along the current path, which will leave the difficult decisions to our children and grandchildren, who will be crushed by the debt created by the excesses of this generation.

As with many aspects of healthcare, to understand the future, it can help to first look at the past. In a report for Deloitte, Greg Scott, Paul Keckley, and Bill Copeland explain,

Two events drove the growth of the industry in the modern era: To recruit veterans returning from World War II, companies used their health insurance coverage to differentiate in recruiting efforts. And in 1972, as part of the Nixon administration, when wage and price controls were placed on employers to control runaway inflation, health insurance costs were not counted against constricted wage ceilings. Health insurance offered by employers became standard fare – first dollar coverage, modest (if any) co-payments, low premiums and deductibles, and large networks of doctors and hospitals from which to choose were common features of many plans. In effect, the workforce was treated to a benefit that mitigated the full gamut of risk from routine office visits and medications to hospitalization for serious medical problems. And Congress granted employers a tax exemption for their portion of premiums now worth $216 billion today.[7]

This makes health insurance a different beast to other types of insurance. "Unlike insurance that covers risk for catastrophes or big-ticket items," the authors explain,

health insurance evolved as a form of comprehensive coverage for everything from minor cuts and routine visits to organ replacement and accidents. It's akin to a hypothetical automobile

---

[7] See: http://bit.ly/deloittehealthinsurance

insurance plan that covers flat tires, not just collisions. And complicating matters, in traditional employer-sponsored coverage, the company pays 75% of the premium so the individual's share is relatively low and the tendency to overuse health services is high. Thus, consumers have little skin in the game. As a result of these structural flaws, health insurance is widely used because it covers everything – and it is expensive for the same reason.

For me, this is both a blessing and a curse, and it is suggestive of what I expect we will see more of in the future. As we as a society shift toward a more preventative model of healthcare, insurers will spend money up front to stop illnesses and diseases from developing so that they do not have to spend more money in the future to treat something that could have been prevented. It is an investment in the future and could save insurers money in the long run.

The only problem is that insurers are hesitant to make these upfront investments because there is a risk that they will invest this money and, then, their customers will switch to a different provider. It is a concern that I can understand, but if the entire industry made the switch to this more preventative model, it should theoretically average out and any losses from people switching policies away from the company should be offset by the gains from new policyholders who are coming in from another provider. It will only work if we see a widespread shift, but I am optimistic, and I expect we will soon see early innovators within the healthcare insurance industry making steps toward a more preventative model. Once these early trailblazers pave the way, the rest of the industry will surely follow.

My Vision of the Future

The healthcare industry is like the majority of other industries, in that it has faced more disruption over the last 10 years than it has at any other point in its history. That makes predicting the future almost impossible, no matter how much experience you have and no matter how forward-thinking you are.

In my books, I do my best to outline the vision of the future that I am working toward, but I cannot make it happen alone. It falls to each of us as stakeholders in the healthcare industry to make it happen. Patients have to demand the future of healthcare if it is to happen, and politicians and lawmakers need to listen to those concerns and to help to facilitate solutions. After all, it is in all of our best interests to focus on predictive and preventative healthcare because it can cut costs and improve our quality of life.

In my first book, *The Future of Healthcare: Humans and Machines Partnering for Better Outcomes*, I outlined how a blend of human insight and technology will beat out either humans or machines acting on their own. This included everything from wearable devices and big data to AI, machine learning, and more. The best option for us as a species is to develop a symbiotic relationship with machines and to use them to usher in the next generation of healthcare.

I aimed to build on that in this book, focusing on how AI and its related technologies can help to create a truly predictive and preventative approach to the way that we look at healthcare. I believe that we have already taken the first steps toward this future, but there is more work to be done before I can relax.

While I was writing this book, I moved on from my previous role at Novartis to join Johnson & Johnson to head their global strategy and innovation in neuroscience. It falls to me to develop strategies to help to manage anxiety, depression, and other mental health issues and to reduce self-harm and suicide. This is preventative medicine at its finest, and I am proud to be able to do it for a living.

But it is still not enough. Predictive medicine is what I live for, and I will not rest until I have seen a sea change in the healthcare industry and a dramatic move toward a value-based, preventative system. That is why, when I am not in the office, you can find me on the road, attending summits and delivering keynotes at healthcare conferences and other events to help to spread the message. I did half of the work on this book in hotel rooms and coffee shops.

There will be another book after this one, and then another and another until my work is done. In the meantime, you can help to do your part to usher in the future of healthcare by sharing this book with your physician and any friends, families, colleagues, and coworkers in the healthcare industry. It does not matter whether we reach healthcare professionals or whether we reach the general public. For these changes to happen, we need to raise our voices. We need everyone to know that the future of predictive medicine is possible. And then, we need them to demand this future from healthcare providers, policymakers, and pharmaceutical companies. If the demand is there, they will have no choice but to cater to it.

There is a lot more work to be done, but I am feeling positive. If you ask me, the switch to predictive and preventative medicine is inevitable; it is just a matter of time. But, for every day that we delay, lives are being lost and irrevocable decisions are being made that seriously affect the quality of life for thousands of patients across the country. If I can help to make the future a reality just a day earlier than it would have happened without me, I will be happy.

That is what gets me out of bed in the mornings. And, I hope I have inspired you to help me with my mission, too. The future is within our grasp. It is up to us whether we want to grab hold of it.

Join the Conversation

Thanks for reading *Predictive Medicine: Artificial Intelligence and its Impact on Healthcare Business Strategy*! I hope it has inspired you to learn more about artificial intelligence (AI) and how it can help to usher in a new era in global medicine.

Whether you loved the book or you hated it, I want to know what you think. Every review helps to make the future of healthcare a reality, so please do take the time to leave a short review on Amazon and Goodreads and spread the word among your friends and family. Together we can make the future of healthcare a reality.

Want to get involved in the discussion? Follow me on LinkedIn, Facebook, and Twitter, or join the conversation using the #FutureOfHealthcare and #predictivemedicine hashtags.

For More Information

emmanuelfombu.com
twitter.com/fombumd
facebook.com/fombumd
bit.ly/fombulinkedin

About the Author

Emmanuel Fombu, MD, MBA, is an internationally recognized authority on the convergence of digital technologies and healthcare. He is an author, physician, and medical futurist with over 15 years' combined experience in clinical medicine, drug development, medical affairs, digital medicine, Business Development and Licensing, research, pragmatic trials, and product lifecycle management strategy in the biopharmaceutical industry and private equity.

His current focus is on how digital technologies can be leveraged to better measure healthcare-related products' real-world effectiveness and value and also to design more comprehensive disease management systems in partnership with digital health startups, payers, and providers.

In addition to his first book, *The Future of Healthcare: Humans and Machines Partnering for Better Outcomes*, Dr. Fombu has authored multiple research papers and abstracts in renowned peer-reviewed journals. As a medical futurist and 2017 winner of the prestigious New York City Health Business Leaders Boldest Digital Health Influencer Award, Dr. Fombu is a champion and advocate for value-based healthcare, personalized medicine, mhealth, nanotechnology, big data, artificial intelligence, machine learning, and digital medicine. He serves as an external advisory board member at the Massachusetts Institute of Technology's MIT.nano project and is an advisor to multiple digital health startups, venture funds, and governmental entities.

Dr. Fombu completed his clinical training at Emory-Crawford Long Hospital and holds an MBA from both Cornell University's Johnson School of Business and Queen's University's Smith School of Business. He also earned a certification in Artificial Intelligence: Implications for Business Strategy from MIT's Sloan School of Management and Computer Science Artificial Intelligence Lab. He lives in New York City.

Index

OTHER TITLES IN THE HEALTH CARE MANAGEMENT COLLECTION

David Dilts, Oregon Health & Science University (OHSU) and
Lawrence Fredendall, Clemson University, Editor

- *Improving Health Care Management at the Top* by Michael J. Urick
- *The Patient Paradigm Shifts* by Judy L. Chan
- *Leading Adaptive Teams in Healthcare Organizations* by Kurt C. O'Brien, and Christopher E. Johnson
- *Management Skills for Clinicians, Volume I* by Linda R. LaGanga
- *The DNA of Physician Leadership* by Myron J. Beard, and Steve Quach

Announcing the Business Expert Press Digital Library

Concise e-books business students need for classroom and research

This book can also be purchased in an e-book collection by your library as

- a one-time purchase,
- that is owned forever,
- allows for simultaneous readers,
- has no restrictions on printing, and
- can be downloaded as PDFs from within the library community.

Our digital library collections are a great solution to beat the rising cost of textbooks. E-books can be loaded into their course management systems or onto students' e-book readers.
The **Business Expert Press** digital libraries are very affordable, with no obligation to buy in future years. For more information, please visit **www.businessexpertpress.com/librarians**. To set up a trial in the United States, please email **sales@businessexpertpress.com**.

www.ingramcontent.com/pod-product-compliance
Lightning Source LLC
Chambersburg PA
CBHW050457190326
41458CB00005B/1329